Mark Cocker is one of Britain's foremost writers on nature and contributes regularly to the *Guardian* and the *Times Literary Supplement,* as well as to BBC Radio. His books deal with modern responses to wilderness, whether found in landscape, human societies or in other species. He has travelled the world in search of wildlife and won a Winston Churchill Travel Fellowship to study the cultural importance of birds in West Africa.

CROW COUNTRY

One winter's night Mark Cocker observed from his cottage in the Norfolk Broads the flight-lines of rooks and jackdaws passing over the house to a roost in the Yare Valley. He then discovered a deafening flock of birds, which rises to 40,000. As he watched the multitudes blossom as a mysterious dark flower above the woods, these commonplace birds were unsheathed from their ordinariness. For Cocker it was the beginning of a journey of discovery, and a realisation that 'Crow Country' is a landscape which we cohabit with thousands of other species and is the richer for these complex fellowships.

MARK COCKER

✦

CROW
COUNTRY

Complete and Unabridged

ULVERSCROFT
Leicester

First published in Great Britain in 2007 by
Jonathan Cape
The Random House Group Ltd.
London

First Large Print Edition
published 2008
by arrangement with
The Random House Group Ltd.
London

British Library CIP Data

Cocker, Mark, *1959 –*
    Crow country: a meditation on birds, landscape and
    nature—Large print ed.—
    Ulverscroft large print series: non-fiction
    1. Cocker, Mark, *1959 –* —Travel—Great Britain
    2. Corvus—Great Britain 3. Large type books
    4. Great Britain—Description and travel
    I. Title
    598.8′64

    ISBN 978–1–84782–286–4

Published by
F. A. Thorpe (Publishing)
Anstey, Leicestershire

Set by Words & Graphics Ltd.
Anstey, Leicestershire
Printed and bound in Great Britain by
T. J. International Ltd., Padstow, Cornwall

This book is printed on acid-free paper

The author is grateful for permission to reproduce
extracts from the following:

'Rook' Words and Music by Sir John Johns © 1990.
Reproduced by permission of Kay-Gee-Bee Music
Ltd/EMI Virgin Music Ltd, London W2CH 0QY.
'The Farmer's Gun' by Andrew Young. © Andrew
Young. Reproduced by kind permission of
Carcanet Press Limited.
'The World's Name' © the estate of W.S. Graham.
Reproduced by kind permission of the Estate of
W.S. Graham.

We wish to give sincere thanks for the following
quoted material: *The Crows of the World*, Derek
Goodwin, (British Museum); *The Act of Creation*,
Arthur Koestler, (Arkana); *In Search of Nature*,
Derek Ratcliffe, (Peregrine); *Biophilia*, Edward O.
Wilson, (Harvard University Press).

This edition is particularly special to me, because my Mum suffers from the eye condition, macular degeneration.
I now dedicate the book to her, with much love.

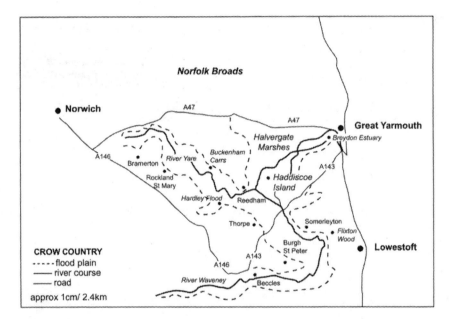

Norfolk Broads

Norwich

A47

A47

Great Yarmouth

Halvergate
Marshes

Breydon Estuary

A146

Buckenham
Carrs

Bramerton

River Yare

A143

Rockland
St Mary

Haddiscoe
Island

Hardley Flood

Reedham

Thorpe

Somerleyton

Flixton
Wood

CROW COUNTRY

Burgh
St Peter

Lowestoft

- - - - flood plain
—— river course
—— road

A146

A143

approx 1cm/ 2.4km

River Waveney

Beccles

The caw of a rook on its homeward way,
Oh! These shall be the music for me,
For I love I love the path of the free.

Eliza Cook, 'I Love, I Love the Free', 1840

This is another of our British birds which is so abundant in almost all parts of our islands, and so well known to our people, and about which so much has been written, that it seems almost presumptuous to suppose we can say or write anything new.

Lord Lilford, *Notes on the Birds of Northamptonshire and Neighbourhood*, 1895

The rook and jackdaw are too well known to need any introduction in themselves, as one need not go far from the centre of the city before seeing one or both species. On the principle that 'familiarity breeds contempt', it is perhaps their very abundance which accounts for our incomplete and inaccurate knowledge of them, in fact as I have frequently learnt to my cost.

Edgar Harper, 'A Study in Rooks', 1904

Author's Note

The extensive bibliography, footnotes and sources have been removed from this edition of the book. They can all be found in the original edition published by Jonathan Cape. Should they wish to know more about the background research to the book, readers are welcome to contact the author directly c/o Random House, 20 Vauxhall Bridge Road, London SW1V 2SA

1

I am awaiting the arrival of night and all that it means in this landscape. Ahead of me lies a great unbound field of stubble sloping gently down towards the hamlet of Buckenham in the Yare valley. At the settlement's southern margin is a tiny railway station, where I stepped down from a train more than thirty years ago on one of my earliest expeditions to this part of the Norfolk Broads. Beyond that steel line is the flat expanse of the Yare's flood plain proper, and from my position on this upper northern slope I gain a sense of the entire valley, the whole flow of its contours, the way that the land dips down then rises again on the far shore like a shallow saucer, like a natural amphitheatre, fit for the spectacle about to unfold.

As day draws into its final hour, our own falling star has dwindled to a lens of brightness on the southern horizon resting in its own bed of lemon and rose light. I watch the clouds being pushed towards it by a biting northerly. They loom overhead like icebergs in an ocean of cold winter blue, and through this interplay of light and darkness arrive the birds I've come to watch.

A long ellipse of shapes, ragged and playful, strung out across the valley for perhaps half a kilometre, rides the uplift from the north wind directly towards my location. The birds, rooks and jackdaws heading to their evening roost, don't materialise gradually — a vague blur slowly taking shape — they tunnel into view as if suddenly breaking through a membrane. One moment they aren't visible. Then they are, and I track their course to the great skirt of stubble flowing down below me.

Along the margins of these fields stand rows of stately ivyclad oaks, where the birds that have already arrived clothe the bare canopy, creating a heavy foliage of black. The whole effect of animal and vegetation reminds me momentarily of the great flat-topped acacias of the African savannah. In the failing light they are mere silhouettes and even the birds that have landed on the ground, wandering among the jagged stalks of stubble, create a simple, fretted chiaroscuro of pale and dark.

My attention cannot rest on the perched birds for long because I'm drawn back inexorably to the drama of the fresh arrivals. The long cylinder of birds, perhaps a thousand in total, has started to coil and circle the sky above the landing ground. They wind up into a single swirling vortex that breaks apart as small groups fling themselves to Earth. It is an extraordinary performance. I am so mesmerised by the flock's sudden and convulsive disintegration that I fail to absorb the trajectory followed by any one individual. But all cease briefly to resemble birds. They become wind-blown rags or scraps of paper. The best I can think of is a moment I saw once in Jaipur, India. Above the city's white-washed skyline floated a thousand small multi-coloured kites all at play in the hot desert gusts on that Rajasthani afternoon. The rooks and jackdaws acquired the same brief power of wild movement, straining against gravity and wind in equal measure.

Even this dramatic show holds me just a matter of seconds because each new development seems more compelling than the last. From the east, from rookeries that I know intimately around the village of Reedham, comes an even larger flock. Perhaps 4,000 birds arrive in a single river of movement and then perform the same wheeling downward plunge of the previous group.

All the while that the visual drama intensifies, their accompanying vocalisations become ever more voluble and excited. Birds on the ground are obviously aroused by the fresh arrivals and send up a great chorus of contact notes. The two species create deeply contrasting but perfectly integrated sounds. The rook's voice is dark, earthy, coarse, tuneless. But in aggregate it possesses a beautiful and softly contoured evenness. The jackdaws meanwhile produce sharp-chipped lapidary notes, like the sweet strike of flint on flint, and in this flinty landscape nothing could be more appropriate. In fact both rook and jackdaw calls seem to come from deep within the Earth, as if it were the valley itself celebrating the onset of night.

The sun has now vanished from the far horizon and the clouds congeal into a single glacial belt of darkness, squeezing the last soft tones from the sky. In these dying moments of the day, when the birds are all assembled, there comes a brief but clearly perceptible lull in proceedings. It happens every time. They fall almost completely silent. Although the first arrivals may have continued to feed, preen, bathe or scrap with neighbours, at day's end they all cease.

They stand expectant, except peripheral birds, which make short silent flights towards the centre of the flock. As they leapfrog their neighbours so they trigger a next wave of outer birds to move nearer to the middle. I

4

can't work out why they do this. Is it some inward quest for security as darkness falls? Or is it simply to get closer still to their neighbours so that they can pick up instantly that last pulse of intention that shapes the flock's final act of the day? Whatever causes it, the process of consolidation is self-exhausting and when there is no inner space left to occupy and the birds have created one huge, undifferentiated mass of black across the field, I know that we're close to the evening's crowning event.

★ ★ ★

It begins almost casually. A single concentrated stream of birds breaks for the trees, the stands of trees that have remained almost unnoticed until this point. Inconsequential while the drama built all around them, the woods known as Buckenham Carrs have grown steadily darker with the onset of night. Now that they have moved centre stage they have become a brooding cavity in the landscape. The birds pour into the airspace above it in evergrowing numbers, and they mount the air until there are so many and the accompanying calls are so loud that I instinctively search for marine images to convey both the sea roar of sounds and the blurry underwater shapes of the flock. It becomes a gyroscope of tightly packed fish roiling and twisted by the tide; it has the loose transparent fluidity of a jellyfish, or the globular formlessness of an amoeba — one that spreads for a kilometre and a half across the heavens.

Even as the spectacle unfolds and captivates me I am restlessly scanning back and forth, slightly on edge because I don't want to miss a thing. I pan back with my binoculars to the original carpet of black across the field, from which the tide of birds first rose. I look back to this initial tableau because it has a magic of its own. For no matter how many thousands of crows have poured away from the grounded mass, the original volume seems as great as ever. This mysterious self-renewing property of the flock persists sometimes for minutes until finally, finally, the numbers start to diminish. Then there is a curious and opposing sense of satisfaction. When the flow ceases altogether you realise that this fantastic tumult involving tens of thousands of birds is finite after all. The thing is compassable. It has limits. It's framed within the natural laws on which you rely. You're not going to float away to some crazy zone where black birds boil up from the Earth for ever.

It brings a momentary steadiness before I try to encompass once more the gathering over the trees. It is no longer a flock of birds. Each occasion I see these protean swirls rise they act like ink-blot tests drawing images out of my unconscious. Sometimes they seem like something you saw before you left the womb, before your eyes first opened, an entoptic vision buried deep beneath the avalanche of waking experience: black dust motes sinking steadily through the gentle oil of sleep. Tonight the flock blossoms as an immense night flower and, while beautiful and mysterious, it always stirs something edgy into my sense of wonder. It is the feeling that in viewing the unnumbered and unnumber-able birds, I am tipped towards the state of confusion which that inchoate twisting swerve so perfectly represents. I freely confess that on the unforgettable occasions when I see 40,000 corvids take flight in one oceanic roar of dark shapes and dark sounds, a part of my sense of joy is the *frisson* of danger the spectacle excites. Quite simply I am at the limits of what my mind can comprehend or my imagination can articulate.

I've enjoyed this moment of the rooks and jackdaws flying to their night-time roost on hundreds of occasions. Over the last five years I've watched the constituent species many thousands of times. For rooks I've travelled as far as Cornwall and Aberdeenshire, Spain and Turkey. I've watched other species roost in Tunisia, in Portugal and in Greece. The moment has never lost its initial thrill and one special ancillary pleasure is now showing it to others and watching their reaction. 'Wonderful,' they often say. 'Amazing.'

This book is all about that moment, about the ritual and the elements of the natural world — the light, the environment, the birds, myself — which create it. It's about how that moment has affected my life and has helped define an entire landscape. It is these things which I call Crow Country.

2

Apparently it's a well-established fact that, aside from death or divorce, moving house is the most stressful experience in our life. There was absolutely nothing unusual about our move then, because it was awful. Initially everything seemed to go quite smoothly. It was right at the very start of the property boom in Norwich during the early part of the millennium. We saw the estate agents on the Friday afternoon and the house had sold even before they could come round on the Monday morning to drive in a stake for the sign. It had gone to a middle-aged couple downsizing at retirement, who assured us that they were cash buyers, so we accepted their offer. It turned out that they were cash buyers — once they had got the money from the sale of their own house.

Perhaps it wasn't their fault. They'd sold that property too, as had the people who were buying their home. But six links down the chain was a maisonette in Woking whose original deeds had failed to specify ownership of the attached garage to its first buyer. He was now selling and the anomaly was spotted

9

in his buyer's search. The company that had first built the property had since gone bust, and sorting out this technical glitch was a six-week money-spinning opportunity for solicitors. In the meantime our life went into freefall.

We couldn't take possession of the new place, nor could we really live in the old. We were just camped out among its four walls. Although 'camping' isn't quite the right word, because it implies a state of relative freedom. Gypsies and nomads camp. They trade possessions for complete mobility, fresh air, peace of mind. We had the worst of all worlds. We had piled all our possessions into 150 boxes, but we didn't have any mobility, because we couldn't move for the trembling ziggurats of cardboard. Our peace of mind was lost somewhere in Woking. It was difficult even to do simple things like cook or go for a bath. We could barely sleep. I couldn't work. In the end it was driving us both crazy.

The madness of moving reached its crescendo on the day that we actually departed for our new life in the country. I remember it vividly; in fact it's one of the few clear moments from the whole period that we can recall. The rest has been blanked out like a suppressed trauma. But that one remaining vision stands for the whole process. Our removal people had been and gone and taken most of the boxes with them in a van, but there was a whole suite of things that we didn't want to trust to the back of a truck and three strapping young men rushing to keep to a strict timetable. Things like our paintings, the television, the video player and an array of brooms, brushes, cleaning equipment and a vacuum cleaner. The last items would be essential the moment we reached the new place, the first implements of attack, as it were, once we'd secured the bridgehead on the other side. But for now, the Hoover and its various tubes ran between the back seat of the car, which was completely loaded with possessions, and the front passenger seat, where my wife Mary was even more securely trapped. In addition to everything else was a computer monitor, the old sort the size of an average television, plonked on to her lap. Elsewhere — on the floor by her feet, in the boot — were the various bits of two more computers, as well as all those infuriating cables that tangle up one with the other.

It was impossible and I decided that something had to give. So we went round to the rubbish skip nearest our home to offload anything we could, only to discover that in the weeks since we'd last visited, the place had been earmarked for development. Where we'd once recycled newspaper and glass there were now half-built homes. Soon, it seemed, there'd be standing room only in the entire neighbourhood. It was one reason we were getting out. But more immediately we had to solve the intense congestion in the car, and insanity proved the perfect laxative.

I got out, marched on to the construction site and found the first workman who would accept a completely free, no-strings-attached computer and gave it to him. He stood there as we waved, buried under the pile of new possessions, while the car gave an audible sigh of relief and we were on our way to a completely new life.

★   ★   ★

The one thing we had truly acquired by moving home was the space we had always wanted. Until that moment it was a life goal that we'd been prevented from achieving by the classic double bind faced by any writer. Being freelance, I'd always worked from home and our requirements had been for more space than was needed by the average family of four. The other side of the equation was the fact that I was a writer. I earned the kind of money that most writers earn. I once calculated that in my first ten years of freelance work I'd averaged about 10,000 per annum. That was before tax. Despite the extremely modest outgoings to the Inland Revenue, ten grand doesn't buy very much space.

At the old house — basically a two-up, two-down terrace — my office had been the box bedroom about the size of a good-sized toilet, into which I'd squeezed two large bookcases, an office-sized filing cabinet and a large desk for the computer. In an attempt to make the most of what we'd got, we converted the loft very cheaply and I'd moved into the roof space. But our daughters were nine and five and we were quickly running out of room again. We needed to get out.

Over five years we'd probably looked through the specifications of thousands of properties and we'd now got it down to a fine art. The two reception rooms and the kitchen downstairs, as well as the two main bedrooms upstairs, were all more or less a given within our price bracket. The meaningful part of the description, the part that might lure us into physically going to view a property, was the exact measurements of the one or two additional bedrooms or, even more rarely, the third room downstairs, for which we were searching. Aside from its location, the issue of moving house turned upon those few score square metres of additional space beyond what we already possessed. It was a deeply disheartening process. And then the Hollies came up.

We looked down the estate agent's sheet of details, listing the rooms and features with their dimensions, in disbelief. It didn't have the three or four bedrooms. It had six, and all of them a good size. One was seven metres long. And there were not just two reception rooms downstairs, but three. In addition there were a utility room, a garden, two bathrooms, a garage. It wasn't a house, to us it was a stately home. It had more than double the space of our old place. (In fact it *was* two houses: one of the previous owners had added an extension equal in size to the original early Victorian property). By the end we were virtually falling over ourselves with excitement. And then all the excitement stopped. We could afford this place. There had to be a catch.

There was. It last belonged to a family of ten and by the time all the protracted negotiations were concluded I think it had become eleven. As part of their fertility drive they had kept all the windows tightly shut and the central heating turned up full blast. In that first autumn when it came time for us to switch it on, it was obvious that the boiler was completely knackered. One of our first expenses was a replacement. Yet in its heyday the original boiler had made the Hollies a province of the tropics with levels of condensation to support the mould and fungal growths you'd expect in the Amazonian rain forest. Some of the microscopic black cultivars in what was once the parents' bedroom are still visible on the walls.

Another room, the large bedroom, had once accommodated three or four children. All down one wall were life-sized images of Postman Pat with Jess the cat delivering the mail, while Thomas the Tank Engine, the scale of a fully operational locomotive, smiled and chuffed alongside them. Downstairs the floors of both the dining and sitting rooms were finished in a high-quality bare concrete. Outside in the garden was a derelict car minus its engine. I say garden. The plot had probably never been touched for a decade. We only found the gate in one of the hedges after several days of slash-and-burn clearance with a strimmer and chainsaw.

Perhaps it was part of the wider madness of that year of moving house that we eventually decided to buy the Hollies. Not that we have ever regretted it. We love it. It's changed our lives. We now realise we owe the previous owners a huge debt of gratitude for their years of neglect. Without that *laissez-faire* style of management we would never have been able to afford it.

★ ★ ★

People often speak of moving house as if this unhinging experience were a natural part of life comparable to the ways in which other species move their homes or change their dens. It isn't. We describe it as *flitting*, as if it resembled a bat's nocturnal flight from one hole in a tree to another. It doesn't. We print little cards and send them to all our friends and relatives that say *so-and-so is on the wing or so-and-so is migrating*. It isn't migration.

Birds are following a set pattern of behaviour that has persisted for 10,000 years, ever since the last Ice Age. In fact it seems likely that, before that time, for millions of years of their entire 150-million-year span on Earth, birds exploited seasonal abundances in this manner. With each fresh interglacial period, when the northern lands warmed sufficiently to host breeding birds, they reacquired the art and science of migration like some cosmic weaver on the great loom of time, picking up a stitch and reworking it at 10,000-year intervals.

Birds have migration hard-wired into their

system. They know precisely where they are going. Don't ask me how they do it — inbuilt sensitivities to the Earth's gravitational fields, to the curvature of its surface, to the stars and to the relative positions of the moon and the sun, whatever — but they do. And to them the unbelievable is ordinariness itself. They do it twice each year. Some do it for ten, even twenty, years. Albatrosses can wander the oceans for five decades.

There is the astonishing story of an Atlantic seabird called a Leach's petrel, a medium-sized, black-and-white species weighing about as much as a small tomato, with long wings and tail. When you get really intimate with it, it has a musty maritime sort of odour like stale fish, and it produces a bizarre vocalisation said to evoke a troll or goblin on LSD. They nest widely in southern Canada and to test their navigational powers two were once taken from their breeding grounds on Kent Island in New Brunswick and were flown to England, where they were released on a Sussex beach. The birds were back in their nest burrows in under a fortnight.

Imagine it. They had been uprooted from their normal daily routines, bundled into a box and placed in an aeroplane, transferred to a car and driven across southern England, experiences that were as foreign to their existence as those of humans kidnapped by aliens with wraith-like bodies composed of liquid gases. The Leach's petrels were then released several days later on an entirely unseen, unvisited shoreline, 4,800 kilometres from where they bred. Yet they found their way back (and presumably in healthy condition, which would imply that they fed as they covered the 350 kilometres each day) in under two weeks. My point is that those extraordinary birds were never in a state where they didn't know where they were, or where they were going. Every centimetre of untrammelled, anonymous ocean, the crushing solitariness of the odyssey itself, was made routine by an infallible instinct for home.

A bird's inbuilt capacity to pinpoint a location works equally well in the other direction — that is, when it's flying not to the nest site, but away from it to the place where it spends the winter. There are examples of pink-footed geese, which breed in Iceland and come to this country in autumn, that have been ringed to allow identification of specific individuals. Some birds have been seen in exactly the same Norfolk field on exactly the same winter day in consecutive years.

It is thought that small birds like warblers — those tiny sheaves of feather wrapped around a thimbleful of blood, a few grams of wing muscle and some twiglets of hollow bone — cover their journeys from sub-Saharan Africa to Europe by stopping at a sequence of places that are known and learned from generational journey to journey. They cross continents but they visit intimate fragments of individual landscapes. The Sahara is not an infinity of sand, it's two days of flying and a wadi here, or a dripping pipe and a few bushes there. Each of these pausing places may be as familiar to it as the tree and the immediate environs of the bird's own nest site.

Take the willow warbler, which winters as far away as the Gulf of Guinea in west Africa. When it first arrives back on the moors of north Derbyshire in early April, and its emollient song — that gently descending octave of silvered notes — rinses the air and surrounds the bird in an aura of vitality that is as uplifting to the human heart as the fresh foliage of its perch; that moment is a triumph of the familiar over the vast and unfathomable unknown. Migration, in a sense, is a miracle not of huge distances, but of small places.

But when humans move house, they don't migrate. They're thrown into turmoil. They've traded all the routines of their past for a blank canvas. There is no handrail of tradition or inherited understanding to steady the journey. There is no homing instinct to guide their passage across it. There is just the unfamiliar and the muddle of the unfamiliar.

We were moving into the countryside just ten miles out of Norwich, but it might as well have been ten hundred. Our elder daughter Rachael hated it. She thought she would never get over the strangeness of the new life, the loss of comforts in her old and the bleak inhospitable character of the house itself. In the event she took twelve months to recover. And to forgive us.

But we were all overwhelmed by the experience. Mary my wife believes it induced low-level depression for months. After five years of intensive domestic reconstruction — cleaning, sorting, tree-felling, demolition, decoration, reassembly, repair, exhaustion and expenditure — close friends now feel able to tell us how they would privately discuss the folly and ordeal of our decision. Perhaps we were cushioned from this same enquiry by self-delusion. Was it in order to maintain that fantasy that we don't now have any images of the raw, unoccupied state of the Hollies when we acquired it, not even the usual before-and-after photos of home improvement? Such pictures, and the opportunity they might have provided for us to reflect on our undertaking, would have been just too unsettling.

Yet we do have one powerful memory to indicate how the comforting routines of our Norwich life had been demolished overnight, and how we had been cast up on the shores of uncertainty by the change of address. On the day we moved it rained torrentially and the three young men heaving the 150 boxes into the Hollies were drenched. Our boxes were also wet and the smell of the cardboard mingled with the cold stale air and the odours of a house locked up and abandoned for twelve months.

Dark skies in winter are expected. But premature gloom in summer has its own indefinable melancholy. It's a product not simply of louring cloud. The half-light arises from the curtains of dense, dripping black-green foliage all around, so that one feels both oppressed and hemmed in. At the Hollies it was worse because a decade of non-intervention had allowed two palisades of leylandii cypress trees to tower over the house at both front and back. In the murkiness of that Saturday afternoon on 2 August 2001, cut off from our recent past and without any clear sense of the future, we were trapped.

It seemed to make the mood in our

21

makeshift lounge all the more ambiguous. We were seated in a line on our old sofa. Wet cardboard soared upwards on all sides. Mary had scavenged some eating utensils from a litter of partially opened boxes, and now fish-and-chip papers with their tell-tale watermark of grease were strewn willy-nilly across the bare concrete floor. Each of us nestled the plate of food in our lap, while two mugs, perched on more damp boxes, were ready to hand for Mary and me. They were filled with the contents of a lukewarm bottle of champagne. It was a very strange moment: a celebration of estrangement.

3

Very soon after our initial operations to make the Hollies habitable we came to realise that we had forged a new relationship not simply with the house, but with its entire surroundings. The setting had, of course, been a major reason for moving into the countryside in the first place. For me, the presence of a spotted flycatcher's nest in wisteria by the front door, and the sight of a marsh harrier directly overhead at the very moment that I first crossed the threshold, were omens no naturalist could ignore.

Yet our first memorable encounters with nature after moving in were with what one might call the great absences of the countryside — the darkness, silence and stillness. In Norwich, like any city, there was always enough ambient nocturnal glow to negotiate the house's interior without ever resorting to a switch. But when the sun sets in the village, the loss of light can be total. At first I found it quite disconcerting to be lying in Mary's arms and not to be able to see her even when my face was inches from hers. This sense of disorientation in the bedroom is often amusing. Several times one of us has woken in the early hours to find the other fumbling for a door in entirely the wrong wall.

It might sound strange, perhaps, but we love the darkness. We love even more its corollary — the vision of a night sky emblazoned with stars, or of a full moon looming over the garden. Sometimes we're so captivated I set up the telescope to enjoy the mountains and craters stippling the sphere's icy whiteness.

All of us are equally entranced by the silence and the stillness of the night. Like a heavy wooden door they close behind us tightly on the affairs of the day, shutting out unwanted intrusion. (Mary says she feels the process begin even as she drives the 12 kilometres back home from work.) Some of the pleasures associated with the Hollies' tranquillity are very specific, such as the sounds of owls after dark. Owls used to call near our home in Norwich, but they were always mingled with the background hum of traffic, the mumbling voices of next door's telly, or segments of conversation from people passing in the street. The wonderful birds still brought a touch of mystery to the city, but at the Hollies their hoots cut their sinuous way through the air with stiletto-like precision and define the silence that enfolds them.

★ ★ ★

It was some time before I began to make wider excursions into the surrounding landscape. There is a small man-made broad about five kilometres from the house known as Hardley Flood. I used to go down in the early evening after work to watch the gulls gather to roost at dusk. The spillage of birds on to the site's shallow waters is really only a minor overflow from the much larger aerial movement that happens every afternoon across this part of the county. The gulls' eastward passage from all points of the compass is one of the great natural rituals at end of day, when their main destination is Breydon estuary, about 15 kilometres downstream. My goal was to see if I could find anything unusual among the gathering rafts of commonplace species.

Success in this department was infrequent but I loved the sense of liberation as I plodded down the track at the water's edge, the sun setting on my right, the raucous notes of gulls drifting off the broad to my left, while overhead a handful of late house martins and swallows seemed embalmed briefly in that warm midge-filled autumn air. Part of the intense pleasure of these excursions, which became a fixed part of the weekly routine in those first months of moving, was the sense that all this was on my doorstep. It was my new territory. I could be writing in the office and then ten minutes later I could be out in an elemental world of water and sky.

The proximity of a natural landscape had been carefully considered when we made the decision to move. Since I write about nature and wildlife, such a habitat was my own kind of work space. Yet the feelings that I encountered as I made my way down to Hardley Flood and, more often, as I walked back to the car with dusk blossoming all around, was far more than simply the pleasure of convenience. Equally the sense of elation seemed out of all proportion to the landscape around me or the experience it afforded. Hardley is a modest fragment of the Broads environment, eclipsed entirely by more famous sites to the north. I found myself pondering on the real reason for these tremendous feelings of well-being.

I tracked back through my past for parallel examples of the same sensation and found myself among my childhood memories. When I was growing up in Derbyshire I had much the same inexplicable sensation of completeness as I walked the area of damp wood and open moor which lay above our family house in Buxton. I always refer to the site by the name of the road on which we lived, but perhaps there was a larger symbolism to that unconscious choice. When writing down my bird sightings for the place in my notebook it was always Lightwood. On the OS map it's called Flint Clough, while the area of heather moorland beyond this spot is close to a tor edge known as Combs Moss. I merged all these places as Lightwood. In conversation it was always Lightwood.

Lightwood was mine. Yet I didn't so much feel ownership. Rather I felt that I belonged completely to it. Birders often feel deep attachment to what's called their 'local patch' — the convenient spot that they visit more than any other. But Lightwood wasn't just my local patch, it was part of my identity. It was my home every bit as much as the bricks and mortar in which we lived. And when I return, it is a pilgrimage to a particular landscape as much as it is a reunion with my parents.

The Yare valley was now exerting the same sort of relationship. We'd opened our lungs and breathed it in. For the first time the Yare valley had enveloped us and sampled our presence. It seemed a perfect consummation.

For only the second occasion in my life I felt truly home.

*   *   *

Landscapes impose their own kind of relationship. In Derbyshire I was used to getting up high on some commanding rock or eminence and surveying the surrounding moors and fields. One of the things I loved most about Lightwood was the opportunity to climb up and sit down, occasionally for hours, and gaze down on the street where I lived. Reduced to the dimensions of a toy, our house and its interior world of childhood preoccupations were placed in their true perspective. It was as if I could see my life from a great height. It brought a strange feeling of power over its trivial affairs.

The Yare valley demanded a massive adjustment. There are no dramatic contours in this place, aside from its fantastical levelness. For the naturalist it imposes a different mode of operation. In the Yare I've got used to scanning the great sweep of flat country and watching things at range. Unimpeded views have come to compensate for the greater distance. I ceased to be concerned with fine detail or being near to things; instead it is the length of observations that counts. Since the creature I'm watching has nowhere to disappear to, what determines the duration is my own attention span. I've learned to be patient and to wait for things to come to me. I set up my telescope and sit in the same place so that it feels like — it is — a kind of ornithological fishing.

In time I've also learned to love a different register of features. Subtly and unconsciously they have become embedded in my experience. For instance it is a first task on arrival at any point of the marsh to scan the five-bar gates and their curious adjunct in this incised landscape, the fence extensions that lean into the dykes at an angle and prevent the cattle rounding the gateway through the water. The complex architecture of posts and cross-beams, which recede through foreshortening in a seemingly interlinked network across the marsh, is the eternal oasis for sparrowhawks, peregrine, merlin, harriers and barn owls that hunt here. I have learned equally to treat each dyke like a hidden valley that you inch towards and, as the full length of the longitudinal strip comes into view, to scan the water quickly for anything that might be resting there.

One other aspect that required a fundamental adjustment was the central feature of this landscape: the river. The Yare is a modest body of water. Looking at its course on the map, you can see that in parts its flood plain is over eight kilometres across, but in comparison with the extensive flats the river itself looks trivial: no more than a single blue wrinkle across an entire face. It's Norfolk's biggest watercourse but it would be difficult to pretend that it's significant in national terms. It's a short river, inherently provincial as well as narrow and slow-flowing. In the 45 kilometres it takes to reach the North Sea after leaving the outskirts of Norwich it falls less than five metres. Twice every day the whole stretch ebbs and flows with the tide and in Norwich it's so saline I've seen cormorants surface with fair-sized flounder.

However insignificant it may seem, it still asserted itself with subtle power. I quickly found that it held sway over an awkward, inaccessible landscape. In the entire stretch from Norwich to Yarmouth it's bridged at either end in the two towns themselves, but in between there is no physical structure across it. I routinely meet people who live on one bank and who have never visited the village opposite, although they may look upon the place every day of their lives. Once I even encountered a couple during a walk at Buckenham who'd lived all their lives in a village on the north side of the river, and didn't even know the name of the village on the other side. The Yare has become a psychological borderline.

Halfway between the two bridges in Norwich and Yarmouth is Reedham where there's a small private ferry, which maintains a long venerable tradition and reflects the historical answer to the Yare's hindrance. In previous centuries there was far more contact between the two sides. On either bank the recurrence of 'ferry' place names — Ferry Road, Ferry Lane, Ferry Farm and various Ferry inns — speaks of a community that looked to the water as the main means of communication. Yet to cross from side to side was one thing; to leave the valley itself was another matter entirely.

I soon found that I too was being hemmed in by the river. Places I used to visit routinely during our Norwich days slipped inexorably beyond reach. Old favourites like the magnificent north Norfolk coast involved a one-way journey of an hour and a half. Much of it was spent mired in Norwich, whose entire diameter had to be crossed each way. I sometimes wonder whether, in my passion for the Yare and its rooks, necessity wasn't the mother of invention. The real origins of my obsession were those regular slow-flowing crocodiles of cars, traffic light to traffic light,

31

through the heart of the city.

One by one, old haunts were abandoned, and strangest of all my 'lost' territories was Buckenham itself, the locality for the rook roost. While it's become the key focus of my present interests, I know it now largely as an exile, looking on from the 'wrong' side of the river. I can see the village and its neighbouring woods just a stone's throw away from our house, but to get there and back is an hour's drive. I can reach Cambridge in the same time. Now I go to Buckenham perhaps three or four times a year.

It isn't just the river making this a place of impediment. All the waters of the valley, over which the Yare exercises its irresistible gravitational hold, hedge me in. Even on my side it's impossible to follow the length of the flood plain directly. To visit a section downstream like Thurlton or Haddiscoe I have to drive almost due south away from the valley, circumvent the single obtruding tributary in this stretch called the Chet, then cut back north to my goal. To reach Haddiscoe, a straight downstream distance of about 11 kilometres, is twice as far by road.

But to walk in the landscape is worse. To the human eye the valley is an extensive plain of grassland interrupted now and then with alluring reed-fringed pools, circled with alder carr or poplar plantations. It seems a gentle, unpeopled, easy place, but its very flatness is the source of the illusion. Bounding every field, and initially invisible to the visitor, is a network of waterfilled dykes. Farmers and wildfowlers have bridged many of them with old rotting planks, known as liggers, but many others have no means of access. And memorising the navigable routes takes a lifetime of familiarity. My walks across the open spaces were often reduced to a tedious tour of each field's inner perimeter, made more frustrating by the sight of my goal and the impossibility of its attainment.

The net result was a reaffirmation of the Broadlanders' old conclusion. This was a landscape fit only for boats. In the Broads sailing vessels are still ubiquitous and their serene passage while I was on one of my cross-country meanderings only intensified any feelings of annoyance. In truth, though, I had little grounds for complaint. The merest glance at the map shows you that the Yare valley is depicted as a network of blue rhomboids. The two-dimensional image of the interlacing dykes reminds me of shattered glass, or possibly — and this may be a simple case of projection — an abstract representation of the mental state induced by walking around the fields themselves.

One consequence of the valley's intractability is that I take a map with me every time I go out. No other landscape has made such a demand. Other places I've lived in or known resolve into a complete mental picture relatively quickly. The different facets link up like parts of a jigsaw, and as the last few fragments drop into their unique, logical place there is that sweet sense of completion. But it didn't happen like that in the Yare valley and, once more, its flatness was implicated in the matter. The absence of relief leaves you with no fixed frame of reference. Depending on the angle of view, places isolated from one another can concertina together and merge. Distant trees that form a far horizon at one spot, in another can rush across the intervening space and graft themselves to a far closer skyline. Church spires or windmills, the only tall buildings in the landscape, shift their locality according to one's own position.

Another factor was the difficulty of access. Different spots remained far longer as a sequence of disconnected fragments. I'd stumble on a plantation or a piece of marsh and feel excited to have located some totally new feature. Only slowly would it dawn on me that the neighbouring building or the configuration of trees, the church tower looming over the top, were all vaguely familiar. The penny would drop — I'd been here before. The difference had been the direction of approach.

Almost perversely, the Yare's recalcitrance became part of its appeal and I found myself working at the business of mental connection. The slow mastery of its geography seemed to increase the sense of belonging. As if to reinforce its tightening grip on my spatial imagination, soon after moving to the Yare I supplemented my chart of the Earth, which had been on my office wall for fifteen years, with a map of the valley. It had become an alternative world.

The most inaccessible part is the triangular block formed by Halvergate and Haddiscoe Island. While the former is the more famous and customary name (it was the site of an environmental struggle in the late 1980s that exposed the corrosive, tsunami-like destructive power of excessive grain subsidies flowing from the Common Agricultural Policy), from here on I'll refer to it as Haddiscoe, simply because it's the part of the whole I know best.

All of the country is low and rolling — its highest point is only 100 metres — but this fan-shaped extension best fulfils Noël Coward's famous dictum on the Norfolk landscape. It is indubitably, resolutely flat, with much of it below sea level. Technically Haddiscoe is also an island, isolated from the neighbouring land by the converging Yare and Waveney rivers and a man-made water channel linking the two rivers. It says something about the long human timeline inherent in this landscape that the dead-straight navigational canal was dug in 1835 yet today is still known as the New Cut.

Together with the two rivers the New Cut completes a three-sided moat around Haddiscoe. Within this level expanse there is just a single straight road going nowhere and it is unpeopled apart from three homesteads. Two of them crouch down in the lee of a steep bank that prevents the Waveney reoccupying its old domain. Their roofs are barely higher than the level of the river and all of them have a laager-like periphery of outbuildings as if defending themselves against the vast nothingness of Haddiscoe's sky. Just to the south of the island, from the bridge at St Olaves, about seven metres high, you can look upstream to the west and the view is uninterrupted for 12 kilometres. To the north, across Haddiscoe's entire length, you can see the giant wind turbines at West Somerton slicing the air with great clarity, yet they are 20 kilometres away.

Such a place requires a major aesthetic

recalibration from its admirers, a transition many don't care to make and they dismiss it as featureless and boring. It is a result of our utter disregard for the beauty of the open plain that this landscape has been disfigured by a regiment of monstrous electricity pylons. It is inconceivable that the Lakes or the Cotswolds would have been violated in this way, yet Haddiscoe seems not even to have been considered a landscape, more a void to the west of the ports of Lowestoft and Great Yarmouth to be treated any old how.

It's true that there are none of the usual constituents of the picturesque. At its most stark, there are very few buildings, no trees and no contours. The stripping away of customary markers does strange things to one's perception. Perspective is flattened out. Features that lie at some range from one another in a horizontal plain are compressed together. Details in the middle distance — a passing boat, a herd of cattle, the brick cylinder of a derelict mill — swim in an indeterminate way, neither getting any closer nor further away, regardless of how long one walks towards them. And if you keep your eyes fixed on this mid-horizon, near things can then take you totally by surprise. Mounds of slub, the thick black mud lugged from a dyke by mechanical digger, break the horizon like a range of hills. Lines of dead thistles erupt from the ground like the broken tops of dead pines in a landscape of snow. A hare jinking away from your feet, bounding off with that odd, intermittent sideways thrust of the hind legs, can seem as big as a deer.

Yet the sheer emptiness of the place can intensify feelings of intimacy with those things that are close. In autumn as I walk the long road bisecting Haddiscoe, the air is filled with dragonflies and occasionally a hunting individual will fly almost at my face. The chitin snapping together as it manoeuvres is like the crackle of electricity, or a firework fizzing before its explosion. Then it settles on the concrete wall, its weightlessness poised on the needletip of its six hair-thin legs. In a few days, weeks at most, you know its life will end. Yet here it is, a scarlet cruciform filling itself with autumn sunlight, savouring the immensity of its existence.

The space all around seems a part of such close encounters. It particularises the moment. Things seem special. I could be wrong. The background conditions may be far more prosaic. It may be that I am simply trapped by the sheer impediment of the river, and I am just making the most of the wildlife that's to hand. But I don't think so. In the Yare valley so many of the things that I had once overlooked or taken for granted were charged with fresh power and importance. It gave rise to a strange and fruitful paradox. I had come home to a place where everything seemed completely new.

4

Rooks are at the heart of my relationship with the Yare. They were my route into the landscape and my rationale for its exploration. Over the last six years I've learned about the birds and the place simultaneously. I cannot now think of one without the other. Yet when I look back it seems bizarre to recall how little they once meant to me. Before we moved I gave rooks no more thought than any other bird. Rather, I gave them less. They seemed so commonplace.

In the Yare it would be true to say I didn't go to look for them. They came for me. It happened several months after we'd moved. Slowly I was conscious of them flying over our house about an hour before it was time to get up. The birds' calls fired down every morning almost without fail. They kept up the barrage for five or ten minutes, the notes clattering on to the road and the rooftops of the village like flakes of tin. A little of the sound came in at the part-opened window of our bedroom and was softened in the sepia half-light of dawn. It filtered through to us as we lay in that twilight state of half-wakefulness, and over the weeks a gradual sediment of awareness must have gathered in my unconscious.

Eventually they dawned on me like a revelation. I found myself sitting up simply to catch the sonorous gravelly voices as they passed. I'd guessed they were in good numbers and that the calls measured the duration of a flock's movements over Claxton. One November afternoon I caught sight of them for the first time. I was in the garden as dusk was falling. Suddenly there was a long silent procession of birds across the sky, a mixture of rooks and jackdaws heading north, presumably on their way to a night roost somewhere in the valley. But where?

Several days later it seemed obvious that I should go and look for the roost site, just as I'd got accustomed to watching the gulls come in at Hardley Flood. It was a mere transference of focus from one roosting species to another. In the way that one tried out another experience simply because it was one more facet of the novelty thrust upon me by a life change, I set off to the river before three, without expectations of it yielding anything of significance.

The first birds were already heading towards the ploughed fields near a big wood, which I now know as Buckenham Carrs, on the opposite side of the Yare. Initially I tried to count rooks and jackdaws separately, but they were so mingled together and they came so thick and fast that I gave up and simply listed them under a single heading: corvids, the generic word for members of the crow family.

The cloud was low and a gentle northerly carried heavy banks of grey slowly overhead, then on across the flood plain towards the southern horizon. I positioned myself with my back to the river and to Buckenham Carrs, looking south and homewards to where the birds appeared in random parties. Loose mobs of several hundred broke into the space above the valley, appearing a few dozen at a time. As quickly as they arrived overhead, I attempted to jot down the total. I don't think I'd ever really noticed how impressive rooks and jackdaws could be in flight.

The two made quite separate impressions. The jackdaws often came in low and hard in small tight knots, a football of birds bounding just above tree height. Otherwise they cruised over, scattered evenly across the sky, wings half closed, each creating a separate, small, missile-like profile and almost invariably completing the short distance to the landing place without a single wing stroke. Then at the last, as they approached their destination — a clump of alders already smothered in roosting birds — they performed a beautiful manoeuvre.

Small groups cohered just before the trees and jinked sideways and up, as if suddenly confronted by an onrushing wall of air. They were like surfers mounting a huge wave and at its apex, with their onward trajectory neutralised by the water's opposing momentum, they were held momentarily still. Then down they came with absolute precision to take a place on a branch or twig among their neighbours.

The rooks were usually a good deal higher when they crossed the Yare. They were less vocal and always flew more slowly. They also lost height in a distinctive fashion. The wings were held at an angle forward from the body and raised above its plane to create a striking dihedral, while the body itself was almost pressed downwards with that weird broken nose of a bill pushed foremost. The posture seemed to spill air from the wings and down they came steadily with curiously light, almost mincing, halfbeats of the wings. Compared to the nippy missile qualities of the jackdaw, the rooks looked stately in their progress.

By the time the flow of birds had virtually

ceased, I estimated about 5,000, although since it was my first attempt to count large numbers it was really a guess. Whatever the true total, it was the largest flock of crows I'd seen in my life. This was impressive enough, but then something miraculous happened.

It was virtually dark. There was so little light, I was barely sure if my binoculars were focused or not. I'd assumed that the great carpet of birds spread across the fields, and down the wires and over the clump of alders, was actually the roost itself. I surmised that the action had ended. Roosting for these birds meant gathering together in a loose aggregation like this. But no.

Suddenly birds started to fly up in a purposeful jet of black shapes spurting for the trees. The movements of some seemed to act as a detonator on the others. Before I knew what was happening the whole host was airborne and swarming towards Buckenham Carrs. When the flock was centred over the wood it started to swirl and twist. The birds were wrenched back and forth as if each was caught by the same conflicting impulses. When portions of the flock turned in unison through a particular angle the entire surface of the wingspan — measuring about a metre on the rooks — was reduced to a single pencil line. The net effect in the quarter-light of dusk was that whole sections vanished and reappeared a split second later. It was as if a tonne of birds was being conjured and re-conjured from thin air.

The flock was as dense as a gnat swarm and yet each dark speck in that fluid drift was a bird weighing half a kilo. Their round-winged shapes were blurred and softened and extended in the dusk light. So at home in the twilight, they resembled an escaping deluge of fruit bats breaking for the cover of nightfall.

Another captivating manoeuvre elsewhere in the flock involved a discrete cauldron of birds that looked as if it were about to break away from the parent body. Yet at the last minute it was as if they were caught in the gravitational field of the main flock. The larger number steadily prevailed, sucking the lesser section back inexorably into its orbit. As it careened home towards the primary group the reunion triggered a separate visual effect. Where they overlapped, the outer birds in each swirl were compressed into a higher density, and this sparked knock-on reactions that eddied through all the birds in a continuous shimmer. It offered insights into the whole airborne manoeuvre. While the flock's globular swirl was shapeless and without purpose, at another level it appeared like an attempt to resolve the spatial discord.

It looked like, it was, a paradox: harmonised chaos. It was beautiful, mysterious and completely unexpected.

The rooks and jackdaws, the birds that I had presumed to know and judged unworthy of a second glance, had gone, unsheathed entirely from any sense of ordinariness. In their place was a vision which was nothing less than magical: the smoke of a genie's lamp in sinuous folds. It was as if I were seeing them now for the first time. The airborne gyre was both guiding star and immense question mark rotating in the night sky. I've been following it ever since.

5

You will have seen rooks. Should you happen to live in the countryside anywhere south of the Great Glen, that deep trench bisecting Scotland from Inverness to Fort William, you'll probably see them, like me, every day of your life. Don't be put off by any sense of familiarity. Rooks are enveloped in a glorious sky-cloak of mystery. They're not what you think they are. But this much we do know.

They belong to a family of birds that the lay person knows as the crows, and which any birder would refer to as the corvids, from *Corvidae*, the scientific name for the family. They're a highly developed group, and are often said to possess greater intelligence than most birds. At one time it was presumed that the corvids were the most highly evolved and the last bird family to appear on Earth. Bird books were arranged to reflect this presumed evolutionary pattern with the most highly evolved, the 'newest' birds, described first. The book then worked backwards through the taxonomic sequence until it arrived at the first and most primitive species. It explains why in many older bird books the corvids appeared in the opening pages, often beginning with the northern raven.

While we no longer hold to this sequence, the corvids are still regarded as highly intelligent. The family is also remarkably successful and its roughly 120 species have occupied the six continents and most of the Earth's land surface outside of Antarctica. Even in the frozen north, the northern raven, the largest corvid on the planet, extends its range beyond the Arctic Circle to the edge of the pack ice, where its uncanny survival skills have earned it the status of culture hero among the Inuit.

In Britain there are just seven breeding representatives of the family. Their official titles are the Eurasian jay, black-billed magpie, red-billed chough, Eurasian jackdaw, rook, carrion crow, and the northern raven. Two of them, the jay and the magpie, subvert the family's usually monochrome impact, and are members of two quite separate genera, respectively *Garrulus* and *Pica*. They're smaller than most of their corvid relatives and even to the least experienced person they are instantly recognisable by their boldly coloured plumage. With its salmon-pink body and chequered wing patches of brilliant azure and black, the jay is a glorious creature, which W. H. Hudson called 'the British bird of paradise'.

Despite the plumage of uniform glossy black, the red-billed chough is another highly distinctive and quite separate member of the family, belonging to the genus *Pyrrhocorax*, the fire crow. This old Greek name honours the brilliant flame colour of the legs and beak, and in this country the chough is further distinguished by extreme rarity. It was once widespread around British coastal cliffs but the inexorable reduction of its specialised habitat of insect-rich coastal grassland has seen the range shrink to a few tiny pockets on the Celtic fringe, mainly in west Wales and a handful of the Inner Hebrides off south-west Scotland. Across Eurasia it is primarily a bird of high montane slopes and huge flocks of choughs can be seen wheeling around the peaks, but at such a range that they appear as little more than dust motes floating in an oxygen-starved ether.

Our four other species are all part of the genus *Corvus* that includes those birds often referred to as the 'typical crows'. Many of the forty species occurring worldwide fulfil the quintessential corvine stereotype — large, abundant, all-black creatures with strong beaks, highly developed powers of flight and omnivorous habits. In the British quartet the raven and jackdaw sit at either end of the size spectrum of *Corvus*, with a raven weighing up to 1.5 kilos, three times the weight of a rook and as much as a grey heron. It's also about as long as a buzzard — roughly 60 centimetres. The jackdaw, meanwhile, can be just a sixth the weight, 250 grams, of its huge relative, and a fraction over half the size.

The jackdaw is also a third smaller than the rook, but it's the one other crow to be found regularly in the rook's company. In some places and at certain times of year, they are constant companions, an inseparability very little explored by avian scientists. Fortunately jackdaws can be instantly recognised in most situations, not only by their small size and quicker, jauntier movements, their staring white eyes and high, crisp, canine yapping calls, of which both halves of the name are onomatopoeic, but also by the lovely pale grey hood that extends like a headscarf from the jackdaw's mid-crown around the sides of the cheeks and on to its mid-breast.

Ultimately the real identification challenge of the British crows boils down to the rook and carrion crow, which together present a test that sometimes stumps the most gifted observers. I've routinely come across birds in late summer that have me scratching my head, even since my rebirth as a rook man. Separating the two reliably depends on the observation of several features.

The carrion crow is a fraction bigger than the rook and about 10–20 per cent heavier. In squabbles for food the larger bird is dominant over its sociable cousin. In many ways it is a more adaptable species and able to occupy the treeless, barren country of the outer isles, where it frequently nests on the ground. The carrion crow also has a rather knotted taxonomy. The birds in northernmost Scotland have pale grey bodies that contrast sharply with the black head and wings. The birds are so distinctive that some people consider these hooded crows, as they're called, a separate species. Whatever their true taxonomic status, the Highland hooded crows' pied plumage is so distinct from the rook's that they are almost impossible to confuse.

The real stumbling block is the carrion crow that is found south of the Scottish Highlands and across the rest of Britain, a range mirroring almost exactly the rook's distribution. Superficially the two species appear all black, but this overlooks a striking iridescence which, although present in both, is stronger in the rook. As a spring adult bird turns in direct sunshine the light bounces off the gloss of the plumage, revealing a deep rich purplish-blue sheen around the whole of the upper body, head and neck. Should the bird raise its wings, the same glorious oil-on-water colours are exposed on the inner portion of both the upper- and undersides. On the forecrown the gloss is tinged with amethyst green, while on the rear cheeks it has touches of reddish purple. Across the whole of the crown and nape the intensity of colour is enhanced by the soft dense feathers, which have a plush velvet-like quality. One might have described the whole bird as beautiful, if it weren't for the bill.

Ironically the weird excrescence surrounding the base of the beak spoils the whole effect of a rook, but enables us to recognise an adult bird instantly. This bare patch allows the species to probe deep into the earth without sullying the facial feathers. Close up, one can appreciate how the skin extends around the eye then along the sides of the bill to the inner edge of the nostril and under the chin, where it is eventually lost amid the scrawny throat plumes. Its gnarled bone-coloured texture reminds me of those hard, squiggly calcareous deposits left by the sort of marine crustacean that one finds on sea-drifted timber or wooden posts at pier heads.

The bare patch draws the human eye to the rook's face and emphasises the imbalance between the long sharply pointed beak and the head. That pickaxe bill is twice the length of the skull and the way that it erupts from its sheath of warty grey suggests the proportions and character of a really big broken nose on a man. It looks like nothing more than a great conk and it often laces our responses to rooks with humour. Perhaps it softens all of our attitudes to the species, in a way that the carrion crow's or the raven's more acutely angled face and beak do not.

Yet there is also something strangely repellent about the skin. The grey scaly character, especially around the eye, has a reptilian quality that seems primitive and ugly. I feel I'm being offered an insight into the appearance of the bird's original dinosaur ancestors. When you watch rooks digging in a field, driving in the bill up to the point of the facial canker, you can almost imagine that these ancient creatures have just struggled up out of the bowels of the Earth straight from the Jurassic.

Unfortunately the fail-safe feature isn't present on all rooks. The birds take two years to acquire the full white-grey patch and prior to that moment the skin is partially or completely sheathed in black feathers. Young rooks that have just left the nest in June and then wander the countryside in roving bands of fellow adolescents are at their most carrion-crow-like and the most problematic to identify.

In this phase of the rook's life one may turn to another useful feature: the feathering on the upper tarsus (leg) and flank, or, in common parlance, the rook's 'baggy trousers'. It would be more correct to describe them as baggy shorts or plus-fours because the feathering surrounds and hides the tarsal (knee) joint but doesn't extend beyond it. To my eyes, however, the detail is more accurately described as an apron of long, loose feathering that surrounds the legs and creates the illusion of pantaloons. These give the rook a strikingly different shape to the carrion crow. The latter has bare legs and a more evenly rounded profile between mid-breast and the top of the tightly feathered shanks. It looks thinner and rangier, while a rook has a softer keel-like slump to the lower foreparts. It makes it look slightly bottom heavy and when it walks it's as if it has to push the legs through all that luxurious plumage, suggesting a slight impediment. The humour of its rustic waddle is compounded by the way that the head and neck snake forwards rhythmically in time with each step.

Once the birds take wing this feature vanishes completely and the only reliable means of separating the two species is the bare patch around the rook's bill base. But gradually I've come to think that there are further supplementary differences between their shapes in flight. The outer five primaries — the main flight feathers — in rook and carrion crow are emarginated, which means that the inner and outer webs of these feathers are indented and narrow markedly towards the tip. On a rook, for example, the outer web at the end of the fourth primary is little more than 3-4 millimetres wide (compared with two centimetres on the inner web at the same corresponding point).

When a rook or carrion crow soars or stalls its flight before stooping or turning, the wing is splayed out at the tip and the outer third of the outermost five primaries emerges like thin fingers poking from the end of the wing. In rooks the fingering is narrower and more pronounced than it is in the carrion crow — a characteristic that reflects the species' far greater tendency to soar and plane on thermals, as the birds love to do in late autumn.

I'm also struck by a small but additional difference in wing shape. It's not always visible and is most often apparent in ordinary flapping flight, such as when rooks progress to the roost at a steady pace, when the fingering on either species is least visible. In this flight mode the wing on a rook looks to me slightly more blunt-ended and has a more swept-back appearance, while the even curve of the rear wing increases towards the last third so that the end looks almost hooked. It's by no means diagnostic, but a corvid in steady purposeful flight with a hook-winged appearance is often a rook.

Finally I mention the most marginal of features, and do so largely because of its magical impact on the rare occasions that I've seen it. It occurs in conditions of really sharp sunlight and arises from the much stronger iridescence in the rook's plumage. I compare it to the strangely disconcerting properties of a photographic negative, when a human figure becomes a spectral cavity in the dark mass of thin air. Likewise, rooks in strong sunshine cease to look black and can seem momentarily, almost radiantly, white. I've never seen the effect in any other corvid, although I suspect ravens may share it. In the words of the Victorian nature writer, Richard Jefferies, 'the bird appears clothed in shining light — it is as if the feathers were polished like a mirror'.

The wings seem the most reflective part of the bird and even in dull evening conditions roosting rooks can show up against the deeper matt darkness of a wood and, while the wings glisten, the body is lost to the background so that a whole flock can become a disembodied swirl of huge shiny black petals, or a flurry of metallic flakes.

Occasionally rooks can, in fact, be white. Like many members of the crow family, they have a tendency towards albinism or a similar condition called leucism where parts or all of the body have pale creamy, sienna or coffee-coloured patches. I once saw a rook where just two feathers — the same corresponding inner secondary on each wing — were white. On another the whole of the inner wing on both sides showed an irregular white patch.

At one time this deviation from nature's intended path was highly suspect and the individuals were treated as powerful omens. The sixteenth-century ornithological writer Edward Topsell called the white crow 'a kinde of prodigy'. In classical times it could portend the outcome of a battle or of a whole campaign. And fear of freaks persisted for thousands of years. In 1768 Gilbert White recorded two extraordinary leucistic birds in a Selborne rookery. Sadly White himself saw them only as eerie milk-coloured corpses nailed to the barn door — the work of some superstitious rustic.

A few localities have become famous for

their 'freak' rooks, and south-west Scotland has produced a string of historical examples. One bird in the mid-nineteenth century at Castledykes, on the outskirts of Dumfries, was a beautiful dusky white with legs of the same colour and delicate light-blue eyes. Another at about the same time had red eyes and was entirely cream coloured, even the beak and legs.

The most striking aberrant corvid I've seen was a jackdaw in a huge roosting group near Hatton Castle in Aberdeenshire. The full moon of that February evening enhanced the ghostly impression of this pearly-grey bird and even in almost complete darkness it stood out with unnatural singularity in the flock like a piece of polystyrene flotsam on a storm wave. Yet as they spiralled overhead, it turned entirely at one with its neighbours, a freak bound into the wider mystery of their night-time evolutions, until the gloom enfolded them all and it was lost to view.

You may notice that I've left until very last the most obvious difference, the feature oftenest invoked by non-specialists to separate a rook from a carrion crow. It is, at once, an inward and fundamental psychological quality in rooks, and yet the most readily visible of all their characteristics: the birds' intense sociability. A carrion crow has a binding social attachment only to its mirror image, its partner. It passes its life as one of a pair isolated from neighbours by a fierce territoriality. The largest congregation one normally encounters of the species is a late-summer band, involving two parents with a handful of offspring.

Rooks, by contrast, live, feed, sleep, fly, display, roost, recreate, fall sick and die in the presence of their own kind. Their whole lives are enfolded in the flock, a collective pattern of their own image — a self-perpetuating inner universe of rook sounds and rook gestures that the birds carry with them, like an enveloping microclimate or a bubble of atmospheric oxygen, wherever they go. In the rookery, those communal bundles of sticks that sway in the bare treetops of March and April, the chicks awaken from the egg with the sound of new-hatched birds in other nests often merely inches from their own tiny orbit of moss-lined sticks. Thereafter life is one continuous shared experience. Their gregariousness means that the solitary rook is almost as abnormal as the bird with light-blue eyes and creamy plumage, and it's what lies behind the venerable East Anglian adage: 'When tha's a rook, tha's a crow; and when tha's crows, tha's rooks.'

I've saved the rook's gregariousness until

last not merely to underscore that it's the layman's most handy distinguishing feature for my bird, but because it was the aspect of the species by which I was most captivated. It was the characteristic that created and bound together the wild bolus of birds turning above Buckenham Carrs. That plume of raw energy was more than simply a latch-key to the unconscious; it opened the cellar door beneath my whole interest in birds. Watching those rooks in their planetary-like revolutions above the trees stirred the very foundations of my birding self, and life has never been quite the same since.

6

You may ask, how could the rook have subverted my whole approach to birds? The answer starts, like birding itself, with the business of identification. You can't proceed with an interest in ornithology unless you're able to recognise the creatures you observe. Identification itself hinges upon breaking a bird down into its constituent parts — the primaries, wings, tail, head, legs, etc. Having deconstructed it into this detailed feather map, one can then attach a specific name to the suite of observed features. In a sense the issue of the rook's flocking instinct was previously important to me only as a characteristic allowing me to recognise the bird.

I've come to realise that even this exercise carries within it a subtle kind of complacency, a curious intellectual sleight of hand, because every time you pin a label on a living creature it reaffirms a sense of mastery over it. The naming of the thing gives you the wonderfully reassuring illusion that you know it. You don't. Sometimes all you have is a single datum. The name. In a bizarre way, the process of recognition can actually be a barrier rather than a doorway to genuine appreciation.

But the real reason why a passion for rooks subverted my whole approach to natural history has to do with the way that the issue of identification feeds into the larger processes of natural history. And we should note that it isn't just ornithology; amateur botanists, entomologists and mammalogists share much the same approach. The very basis of a day's natural history is going out into the field and seeing what you can find. It appears a highly open-ended process. There seems to be no obvious prescription, but subtly, unconsciously perhaps, one is governed by a set of tacit expectations. You wouldn't, for instance, spot a blue tit or a bed of nettles in the first few paces of your excursion and remain studying that until it was time to go home. In the case of the blue tit you'd raise your binoculars, glance at it, confirm its identity, and walk on a few seconds later.

The underlying factor governing this response is the scarcity of the species in question. Unconsciously, all amateur naturalists on field excursions are questing for the unusual. This doesn't mean that there isn't great satisfaction in the matrix of inevitable background conditions — the fresh air, the natural landscape, the sensation of sun or wind on face, the simple pleasure of limbs moving freely in the act of walking, the sense of liberation that results merely from being out of doors. Equally the nature of that special encounter can be expressed in many different ways. It may be an animal or plant species that isn't inherently uncommon, but it's present at a strange time of year, or in a habitat that isn't typical. Seeing a tern, a bird of the seashore and open water, floating gracefully above the middle of a busy city street has a kind of specialness and merits a level of attention that it would not draw from you in its more usual setting.

Unusualness or scarcity can become the only or the overwhelming factor in one's natural history, to the point of obsession. Twitching, the process of travelling long distances to see birds that are extremely rare, is a way of contriving the extraordinary in your wildlife encounters. But it is really only an extreme version of what all of us are doing. Because, as I say, the underlying goal in any outing is to have an encounter of some meaning. Of course it doesn't always come off. Many is the time that you go out and see nothing exceptional. But it's those 'failures', those blank days, that lend significance to the encounter of meaning.

If you like, our encounters of meaning are the edited highlights from the excursion, the parts that lift up your spirits for the rest of the day. They are the moments of the outing you might relate to friends or family once you return. On many of the evenings when I go out in search of rooks the conventional notable bird, the encounter which is always committed to the notebook, alongside all my observations of corvids, is the barn owl.

It is a perfect species to help explain my argument. Even at the most simplistic level a barn owl seems the antithesis of a rook. One is common, black, noisy, gregarious and diurnal. The other is scarce, ghostly, silent, solitary and nocturnal. To see the two birds together during the same short walk down the back fields is significant in itself, a changing of the guard between the things of day and those of night.

Barn owls are inherently noteworthy because they're predators. Their very ecological location at the summit of the food chain means that they are intrinsically low in number. In that imagined pyramid of life, with its broad base of lower producer organisms supporting ever more evolved forms, the barn owl is the capstone. In Britain the species is even more special than its predatory status implies. Habitat destruction and loss of the rural architecture that once provided this specialist hole-nesting bird with its usual breeding sites mean that barn owl numbers have slumped to just a few thousand pairs.

They are also, one can easily argue, engaging simply because they are nocturnal. Encounters between a bird of the night and a diurnal primate are shot through with significance. Often they float towards me out of the dusk, oblivious of my seated presence on the bank, and are so intent on hunting that they come to within a matter of a few metres. There seems to be a type of meaning even in this momentary proximity, because barn owls have acquired an instinctive fear of humans over the millennia. To find a passageway through the bird's enveloping aura of watchfulness, until the owl finally swallows my presence down with those human-like dark eyes, is tinged with a sense of thrill.

These moments of magic in natural history have a special almost suspended quality. Ordinary existence, the processes of time, seem on hold or frozen. The more powerful the encounter, the more outside normal experience it appears to be. These occasions offer a way of plucking meaning and value from the day. In a sense natural history is a game of chance, pitching time and skill against fortune. When we have success it feels like a benediction, and if this happens several or many times in one day, then that singular twenty-four hours can become a hallowed fixture in a life, to be recounted or written about as if it had sacred import. It's in this way that I think natural history can serve as a metaphor for life itself.

Until my encounter with the rooks this was the very basis, the core of my natural history, a hoping and a daily quest for these encounters, which would lift my spirits and give fulfilment to my excursions. Every day I would start afresh with my pockets empty. And at the end of each day I would remove the day's takings from the till.

With the rooks it was different. Earlier I said that no naturalist would set off on an outing and halt at the first blue tit or the first bed of nettles which he or she encountered. With the rooks that is precisely what I did. I focused on one of the most common, ubiquitous birds of the British countryside. Natural history was no longer calibrated to scarcity, nor was it a loose, open-ended quest. There was no chance of taking a reckoning at end of day. My gains were cumulative. The process continued from week to week, even, eventually, from year to year. I'd set myself the challenge of understanding why rooks behaved as they did. What drove the creation of their flocks? Where were they coming from to form the roost? Why were they coming? What mechanisms triggered each stage?

To understand as much as I could about that swirl of birds over Buckenham Carrs, my natural history had to become tighter and more structured. My relationship with the one species had become an evolving narrative, the bird's mysteries a constant puzzle. It meant that every tiny observation could potentially be an addition to or modification of the whole picture. I made excursions with single, express goals in mind — to work out the number of birds or nests in one spot, or log a series of timings, or observe a fragment of behaviour. Filling in the parts of the jigsaw in this way could be a very hit-and-miss affair. But one strange consequence was that even if I saw nothing at all during an outing, it could have a satisfying outcome in the sense of revealing rook behaviour a little more clearly.

Classic examples of this were my many excursions to delineate the geographical area of recruitment to the Buckenham Carrs roost. I was fascinated by the way other people who had studied corvid flocking behaviour had been able to work out, apparently without particular difficulty, the area from which a roost recruited its members. Rooks in winter use their breeding location, the site of the rookery, as a gathering point before departing for the place where they will spend the night. Between the rookery and roost are conspicuous flight lines, like the one that passed directly over our house.

To plot them all necessitates a sequence of outings to the surrounding rookeries to observe the route taken by their occupants towards late afternoon. The compass bearing of their dusk flight should confirm to which roost the birds are heading. Unfortunately I found that it seldom worked out as neatly on the ground as it does in theory. The hour at which rooks gather in the rookery prior to their journey to the roost varies according to distance from the roost itself, or possibly according to mere whim.

They may just visit early in the afternoon and then make a staggered, circuitous meander towards their nightly sanctuary. To ensure that you can track their last movements on, say, a December evening might involve waiting by a rookery from two o'clock onwards or even earlier. A two-hour wait on a cold winter's afternoon until a flock of birds decides it's time for bed is hardly the most engaging experience. Nor is it without hazards. Sometimes the rookery is close to houses, and an adult male loitering without apparent purpose, armed with binoculars or telescope, can look remarkably suspicious. Occasionally I've moved off simply through embarrassment. I have to confess that, to this day, five years after I started, I don't know for certain the exact boundaries of the area from which all the birds converge on the Buckenham Carrs roost.

I found that the next-best thing to watching by each rookery in turn was to find some high ground, preferably away from houses, that intercepts the presumed journey which the birds will make, then to sit and wait at this halfway point. Unfortunately south Norfolk isn't blessed with too many high places and I started to envy those who had done their studies in Cornwall or Northumberland, where large panoramas of the landscape could be obtained from a single high hill.

One place where I went to examine recruitment to the Buckenham Carrs roost was a slight vantage point about 10 kilometres south-west of the Yare valley. At a mere 40 metres above sea level this imperceptibly raised tumescence in the Norfolk flatlands was, in fact, the highest point in the whole area. On the map the spot seemed to intercept the route which rooks would have to take from five rookeries that were further south. The place therefore had strategic value for me, but it was beyond the periphery of what I considered my core area.

The main reason I don't go there is because it lies within a large swathe of the county's prime farmland, and agricultural intensification has reduced its avifauna to a bare minimum. In my previous life I would never have dreamed of going there. In parts it is virtually birdless. There is small hope there for encounters of meaning.

'Lost' or 'forgotten' Norfolk doesn't convey it, because the words imply that it is in need of rediscovery, or that one day it will be remembered. 'Abandoned Norfolk' is my preferred description because it's a part of that cavernous, deadened heart of south England which now runs more or less uninterrupted from Norwich all the way to Bristol. More than half a century of chemical farming has drained it of much of its wildlife.

The domestic gardens around the houses are invariably the most diverse portions, and the odd rookery is often the only conspicuous community of wild birds within it. In Norfolk the obduracy of water has been the saving grace for the wildly beautiful north coast, the Broads and the river valleys. But the clay plateau running from Norwich to the Suffolk border has probably been farmed for over 3,000 years.

Whenever I venture into this section the overwhelming impression flowing from its regularity is of industrial manufacture. A place that is largely managed by machines has itself become mechanical in character. A pumped-up greenness is at the heart of the artificiality. Ironically, the colour we've come to associate most with the English landscape — and with the social movement that holds the environment dear — is the one that speaks most eloquently of its decimation. Green without relief is unnatural. Stippled, mottled or subtly graded are all nature's models. Gerard Manley Hopkins in a poem of thanksgiving for 'Pied Beauty' wrote,

Glory be to God for dappled things . . .
Landscape plotted and pieced — fold, fallow, and plough.

But the prospect of an England of unrelieved fertiliser green is the chromatic equivalent of another nightmare vision, Rachel Carson's bleak evocation of a birdless world, *Silent Spring.*

Don't get me wrong. I don't despise this portion of Norfolk. Far from it. I still love it, as one continues to cherish the thought of a friendship or relationship that's long turned sour. It has pockets and moments of enormous beauty and on this occasion I came across a green lane where old coppiced ash, hazel and maple fountained upwards and linked arms overhead to create a long cavern of yellow and russet foliage. As I plouted through this magical corridor I felt I was on my way not just to the Middle Ages, but to the Neolithic.

It was late November and a glaze of ice skated across the puddles along the wide lane. In the ditches either side were runnels of water escaping its gentle incline. The sound of that shrill trickle had the impact of a cold drip down the back of my neck. (Tracing a delicate wriggle of blue on the map, I realised later that it marked the Yare's southeasternmost watershed. A mile further and the trickles all flow south to the Waveney.) The lane proved to be a very old feature indeed. It was marked as a sizeable thoroughfare in the eighteenth century, featuring on Faden's 1797 map of Norfolk, and was probably already ancient and well-worn then. I found coppiced ash stools that were four metres around their girth and were still throwing out wild hedgehogs of black-nibbed new growth. One huge oak looked four or five hundred years old and from its middle branches a little owl bobbed and glared as I approached, then bounded along the lane, vanishing down the tunnel of gloom.

That same afternoon — at 15.43 exactly — I saw three rooks. They were heading south-west, in the opposite direction to the one I'd presumed and hoped they might take. God knows where they were going, but it was *not* Buckenham Carrs. But even this paltry observation was an achievement of sorts. It showed that there was no recruitment from the rookeries further south. Or, at least, I had established incontrovertibly that there was none in that early part of the winter, or that their route was not the one I'd presumed. A tiny fragment had been gained. But it would probably take several more fruitlessly productive excursions to establish the full picture.

7

It was one thing to drive out into the local countryside I didn't normally visit. It was no more than a modest expenditure of time and effort to stand for a couple of hours and see nothing but three rooks flying in the 'wrong' direction. In fifteen minutes I could be home and all would be well. In fact rooking in autumn and winter has an inbuilt convenience from the point of view of domestic harmony. Most of the key behaviour occurs at first light or last. In between, a naturalist can spend much of the day cutting and laying tiles, emulsioning walls, digging the flower-beds, like any ordinary person recently moved to a run-down cottage.

But driving all the way from Norfolk to Dumfriesshire to examine a small aspect of rook behaviour is a different matter. It's a round trip involving a cool 1,100 kilometres, about sixteen hours non-stop on the road. It's a minimum three-night stay away from home. It's £200 of expense. When you're forty-five years old and the adventure of travel has palled a touch, then several evenings confined to a room in a rural B&B are not full of romantic possibility. They're tedious, the evenings somewhat lonely, a blend of hot drinks with little plastic cartons of milk, of lying on the bed flicking the remote control, of ringing home to check all is well.

But when all this happens and you fail to obtain the missing detail you'd hoped for — when you can drive down the motorway for 500 kilometres and your mind is free to reflect on the jigsaw piece you didn't find — it's a waste of time of a different kind. It can engender the feelings of emptiness that lead you to question what on earth you're doing. Rooks may have become my first love but it isn't a relationship without its phases of doubt. My worst moment came just as the midwinter sun was going down on a wind-lashed hillside in the middle of nowhere.

★　★　★

It's a tale of blank despair and ultimate redemption and it all came about in the winter of 2005. Any rook man is ultimately obliged to visit Dumfriesshire. It's the place where rooks have been surveyed most systematically and over the longest period. The father of the process was Hugh Gladstone, author of *Birds of Dumfriesshire*

(1910). At the turn of the last century Gladstone mapped all the rookeries in the county and traced evidence for some of them back to the 1650s. This was remarkable enough, but his efforts were self-perpetuating. Dedicated rook men like Derek Skilling picked up the baton and in the last fifty years have repeated Gladstone's county-wide census four times, with two other partial surveys. Skilling and his colleagues have made Dumfriesshire's one of the best-known rook communities in Britain.

But it was something in Gladstone's original book that first fired my imagination. Writing on the patterns of rook-roost behaviour like those I was studying in the Yare valley, Gladstone quoted a passage from a letter sent to him at the time he was completing his book. 'Mrs Pollock writes me,' he noted, 'that in about 1866 'the Rooks had innumerable nests in the old wood (Dalswinton). On a summer's night (put early to bed!) I have lain by the nursery window, watching them flying home from the White Hill; the sky would be black with them, their flight overhead would occupy at least an hour and a half — a wide stretch, apparently one hundred and eighty yards. It looked like a river.''

His correspondent was the daughter of a

wealthy landowner who lived at Dalswinton House, a large country pile just to the north of Dumfries in the Nith valley. Her account proved that she was witness to something extraordinary. Although one may surmise that her description involved a degree of exaggeration — after all, she was remembering events that may have occurred forty years before she put pen to paper to correspond with Gladstone — a river-like flock that took ninety minutes to pass the house was a major corvid gathering.

Mrs Pollock's fragment of information happened to interlock with another paper I had that described the results of a nationwide survey of Scotland's winter rook roosts. This second document, published in 1971, established that a nightly flock of 10,000 birds gathered in the village of Dunscore. It seemed remarkable to me that, as the crow flies, Dunscore was just seconds from Dalswinton. Both of these small hamlets were about ten kilometres north of Dumfries. If the roost still existed, it suggested that Mrs Pollock's 1866 river of birds up the Nith might just possibly have followed the same routine for nearly a century and a half.

Even if the close proximity of the roosts was a matter of coincidence, I thought it valuable to check whether the Dunscore gathering still occurred. To find this one alone, almost thirty-five years after it was first recorded, would be proof of remarkable site persistence. One of the aspects of corvid behaviour which fires my imagination is the length of time, the sheer span of rook lives, that knowledge of a particular roost is passed on from one generation to the next.

Unfortunately I made a big mistake on the night of my visit. On the Ordnance Survey map you can see that a single tall hill lies almost equidistant from Dalswinton, on the east side of the River Nith, and Dunscore on the west. It seemed an uncanny omen that the spot was called Crawston Hill. 'Craw' or 'Craa' is a Scottish name for rook. Where else would I sit but on its summit? I could overlook the roost at Dunscore, but keep a watch for any sign of Mrs Pollock's nursery visions from 1866. In fact, the name 'Crawston' has no connections with the bird at all. (I'm grateful to the staff in Dumfries Library for subsequently showing me that it derives from the surname of a medieval family, the McRaths. In 1625 Crawston Hill was spelt Makcraweshill.)

By the date of my visit in January 2005 a succession of Atlantic depressions had ravened across middle Britain like wolves. In some parts of western England and Scotland

78

about 22 centimetres (c. nine inches) of rain had been dumped in a matter of hours. Earlier that day as I'd driven up the M6 motorway I'd crossed the River Eden. It spanned almost the entire width of the bridge, a dull turbid sheet muscling down-stream, where it had just inflicted on Carlisle the worst floods for several generations. At some houses the water had reached the upper floor.

A second depression was just then careering wildly into Dumfriesshire as I drove towards Crawston Hill. I parked at a small farm on the southern flank and asked the sleepy-eyed farmer if I could walk on his land. With the typical generosity of country people, he nodded quick assent but I could see the look of stark puzzlement in his thin, grey-cold face. Why had an Englishman travelled from Norwich on this raw night to watch 'the crows', as he called them. Already the project was starting to feel a little shaky.

Gusts banged at the aluminium stalls where the cattle munched nonchalantly, cocooned in that soothing ancestral blend of warm straw and sweet bovine reek. I almost envied them their simple animal intimacy. Out on the bare hill I was surrounded by vast space and wind. A relentless hiss of air shut down my senses. I could see nothing for the tears streaming from my eyes, nor hear anything but the sharp hack in my own breath.

Overhead cloud banks sailed across the Scottish Lowlands and doused the light, leaving it prematurely dark. The climb was a blustery breathless gloomy slog. At the end I realised too late that there would be no single Cyclopean panorama involving both locations. A small ridge, undetectable on the map, partly cut off my view of Dunscore and the more I positioned myself to overlook Dalswinton, the less I could see of the other site. There was no time now to backtrack and my timetable gave no opportunity to repeat the watch the following night. The success of the whole journey north, 600 kilometres over forty-eight hours, hinged on what I saw in the next hour.

Instantly I had to halve my potential return. I would have to look just one way or the other, and since the paper on winter roosts was the more recent information, albeit more than three decades old, I chose the clearer, if still impeded, view over Dunscore in preference to the Victorian idyll at Mrs Pollock's Dalswinton.

But worse than the lack of full vision was my inability to hold my binoculars steady in the constant gusts. My shakiness in the farmyard rapidly developed into a full-blown sinking sensation. I tried to rest my arms on the wall and clench my body against the wind. But it was hopeless. Then I tried squatting down with my back against the wall. Briefly I saw a small swirl of corvids tossed up over Dunscore, but when they crested the hilltop and came in range of the wind's full blast they were instantly scattered like gunshot.

The rain-soaked lichen on my stone seat was imprinting an inverted replica on my arse and the cold had acquired a rat's relentless incisors. My fingers were soon burning hot-frozen. I couldn't work the binocular focus wheel. It had gone stiff. Not that it mattered. There was nothing to see. Nothing moved. The cloud had massed in a solid lid just above the hills and it was virtually dark. It felt like one of those thousand other moments in my rook quest when things had gone wrong. Only this time I was a very long way from home and the consoling cup of tea or glass of wine with Mary.

There would be no discovery tonight. No hard-won piece of the jigsaw would drop into place. I was alone on this windblasted hillside in the middle of nowhere and I began to wonder why. What had I hoped to achieve and why on earth had I bothered to climb up here? I was annoyed mostly because at the back of my mind I knew there had been another hope that was even more vague than the false etymology of Crawston's name.

The spot was within spitting distance of Ellisland Farm, which the poet Robbie Burns had bought in 1788. In his poem, 'The Cotter's Saturday Night', Burns had written:

November chill blaws loud wi' angry sugh;
The short'ning winter-day is near a close;
The miry beasts retreating frae the pleugh;
The black'ning trains o' craws to their repose:
The toil-worn Cotter frae his labor goes —

These beautiful slow-flapping lines of poetry had come back to me as I drove the short distance past Ellisland to Crawston, almost as if they were a further omen of impending success. I particularly loved the way Burns had captured how corvid flight lines are unconsciously embedded in the mental furniture of nightfall. He'd also glanced at the rook's importance as a natural chronometer for the agricultural day. From Crawston's summit one might just be able to pick out Ellisland in the far distance. How perfect, I thought, to see the descendants of his blackening trains o' craws re-enact his poem more than 200 years after he'd written it. No true scientist would have given it a second thought but I did and at the last minute I spliced it into the list of the day's objectives.

All these significant threads of connection — the Dunscore roost, the Dalswinton river of birds and Burns' craws all from a hill called Crawston — had suddenly come together. As if by magic they had seemed to be weaving themselves into one triumphant dusk spent rooking on the hill and I gave in to the possibility. But on that cold-burnt spot my imagined world disintegrated into make-believe. The whole thing had failed completely and I headed down for the car.

It was now dark and I'd seen barely a handful of birds, but on a whim I decided to put off the retreat to my hotel for a few more minutes. From Crawston I could see the tops of the highest trees at Dunscore but not the body of the wood itself. Just possibly . . .

I wanted to look at the exact spot named in the 1971 paper where the roost was said to be. So I drove through the village and out again and there was the site and there suddenly were the birds, dipped down below the ridge in a way that meant I might never have seen them earlier.

Thirty-four years after they had been recorded and they were still there, still coming in large numbers to the same small plantation. In 1971 I was eleven years old with a million possible futures ahead of me. Of all of them I had chosen birds. Then rooks. And here I was. And here were they. A long looping windstretched line, mainly of jackdaws, which maintained an irrepressible *jak-jak-jak-jak* conversational merriment. It created its own sphere of joy in that acid-cold night. It was wonderful and I felt exultant.

High winds always seem to intensify the mood of a rook-jackdaw flock, but this smoke twist of corvids positively revelled in it. I'd lose sight of them and their chaotic rubble of stony notes was caught and flung off by the gusts. Then with any lull they would come back, the sound expanding incrementally with their return, to the same window of sky immediately above the road and over me. In the oblique glow of the car headlights they were reduced to black fruit-bat-like shapes, but I could differentiate the smaller, neater dove-like outline of the jackdaws from the ragged sweep of the rook wings.

The wind teased them out into one long rope of birds, perhaps 2,000 in total, and while the line would bulge and twist, the point where I stood seemed to exercise a curious irresistible magnetism for them. Slowly the bird rope seemed to be hauling itself into a single mass over my head, and no matter how hard the wind smashed at them, ripping at the edges of the flock and lashing them wildly outwards like witches' hair, they were irrepressible. And back they came.

I watched for ten, fifteen, minutes with this wind caravan of birds swirling and dipping towards me. At times I wondered if they could see me — a strange, illuminated figure looking up into the night from that wet black road, alone, car door flung wide open where I'd leapt out, engine running, headlights still tunnelling vacantly into the dark. I stood there and drank the moment down. I had a weird sensation that they were doing it all for me and had I not been there as witness, no one would have seen a thing.

8

In the time that I've been a rook-following man there's been a wildlife programme on television that was searching for what its producers called the 'bird brain of Britain'. The species which came out top was the rook. Its winning performance was filmed at a service station on the M4 motorway, where the local birds have learned to raid the waste bins around the car park after motorists have dumped their fast-food wrappers and leftover scraps.

Although rooks elsewhere have been recorded as flying down and landing inside the bins, a hazardous and tricky manoeuvre for such a large species, the M4 birds have acquired the art of pulling up the black plastic bag with their bill. As an individual lifts out a section it clamps the small pleat of plastic under its foot and repeats the operation until the contents at the bottom are steadily hauled within reach.

The trick is typical of the many survival skills that rooks deploy in pursuit of their highly catholic diet. Birds have been known to skim edible foods off the top of rivers or dive for fish just below the surface and catch them in their feet osprey-style. In the garden they'll haul up strings holding lumps of fat or threaded with peanuts, intended only for tiny acrobats like tits, and then eat them from their perch. An equally remarkable feat, possibly achieved after observing the tits, is to hang suspended from the bird-food holder itself and take the nuts directly through the wire mesh.

A further measure of intelligence is their ability to store surplus food as an insurance against hard times. The behaviour is wide-spread among corvids and I remember once watching a raven bury a small fish it had picked up at a reservoir edge, then replace the divot of turf it had dislodged in the act of concealment. By far the most advanced and easily observed example of food storage by British corvids involves the Eurasian jay. In the autumn, adult birds gather and hide away thousands of acorns, usually pushing them a few at a time into small holes in the soft earth.

It's the moment in the year when jays suddenly become conspicuous. They cross the autumn sky with that strange, slow, stalling, butterfly flight-action, and as they go you can actually see the sublingual pouch in the throat bulging with its cargo of acorns.

Jays have a wonderful memory for their caches, sometimes digging down through snow to relocate them.

Rooks' efforts are modest by comparison but there are reports of them burying acorns, walnuts and pine cones. The behaviour appears to be locally common in parts of Scotland and it gives substance to an old piece of Aberdeenshire vernacular for self-seeded trees. Farmers sometimes describe these adventitious sproutings as 'craw-sown' — rook-sown.

A further measure of rook adaptability is the capacity to catch and kill other animals whenever an opportunity presents itself. They will eat live mammal prey up to the size of a hamster and birds as large as young chickens. They also routinely wander along the strand line for the tide's leavings, and an interesting technique is to fly above coastal rocks with sea urchin, crab or mollusc, then repeatedly drop it until the shell is broken.

Rooks will sometimes supplement their diet with the eggs from other nests. Ground-nesting waders like lapwings are occasional victims and the bird's alleged depredations upon pheasant and partridge mean that rook corpses routinely swing from the barbed-wire fence or the gamekeeper's gibbet. My own hunch is that the nest-robbing charge has been overdone. Most records arise in the breeding season when parents are under pressure to deliver protein to their hungry offspring. Chance encounters with other birds' eggs are just one more example of the species' opportunism.

Occasionally, however, their resourcefulness is welcomed by the farmer. The Victorian ornithologist William Yarrell reported the occurrence of a locust swarm near Craven, Shropshire, that was demolished with the arrival of tens of thousands of rooks. He also described how the mountain vegetation on the slopes of Skiddaw, near Keswick, was at risk of devastation from an enormous outbreak of some form of caterpillar. Once again the rooks rode in like cavalry to the rescue. The most notable of these avian morality tales involved a well-documented plague of voles in south-west Scotland. In 1891–93 an area of upland country running for about 100 kilometres in length and sixteen in width was devastated by a rodent infestation of biblical proportions. Once again it attracted large numbers of rooks which killed and devoured the pestilent voles in their thousands. A committee appointed to inquire into the origins of the plague concluded that over-zealous control of predatory birds like rooks may have been partly responsible in the first place.

A variation on the theme of the sudden glut is the modern rubbish dump. Rooks are freebooters on waste tips and at the site in Burgh St Peter, the village on the eastern edge of my Yare territory, the birds form a smothering black mob. To harvest the spoils, the flocks choreograph their movements with the bulldozer's mechanical shunt back and forth through the heaps of rubbish. When the sun shines to pick out the rooks' glossy iridescence and highlights the rainbow sweep of colour among the rotting detritus, I find these scenes of irrepressible life and lavish waste intensely poetic.

I imagine it was this same faintly macabre spirit that inspired another rook-watcher, the well-known writer and naturalist of Great Yarmouth, Arthur Patterson, to report birds feeding on the putrid carcasses of dead dogs slung into Breydon estuary in the early years of the twentieth century. One of Patterson's correspondents saw more than twenty rooks feeding vulture-style as they cleaned up the corpse of a dead sheep in the winter of 1906.

I've never seen it myself but the eyewitness descriptions of rooks scavenging a carcass lead me to infer a far more ancient and resonant scene. Our Mesolithic ancestors were accustomed to place deceased relatives on special excarnation platforms where natural predators could pick the bones clean, before the remains were taken to be buried in a barrow or cairn. I can just imagine the rook flock that chanced upon the same easy pickings, smothering the raised corpse in a blanket of dark wings and excited calls.

★ ★ ★

The various feeding strategies of rooks listed above are a measure of the species' flexibility, enabling it to capitalise on momentary circumstances, but they have had little bearing on its evolution and history. At the basis of the species' ecology are the items which constitute the core of its diet, the insects and arthropods found in the upper topsoil. A rook's stiletto-like bill with its gnarled hilt of bone-coloured skin is perfectly adapted to feeding in the first 5–6-centimetre layer of turf. Its last few millimetres are mainly cartilage and well supplied with nerve endings. Just watch them when you next see a flock in the fields; the way they work the ground outstrips the spadework of any professional gardener. The bird waddles along and then seemingly at random it punches the beak down, often with considerable force and sometimes shifting the body right round the better to prise open a cavity in which to search for invertebrates. The technique has acquired a name, *Zirkeln* — from the German word *zirkeln*, 'compass points' — that is translated as 'open-billed probing'.

British studies of the main spring prey taken through *Zirkeln* indicate that small worms (not the big fat pink garden species which fascinate small children) are the critical component, such as *Lumbricus terrestris, Allolobopbora longa* and *Allolobopbora caliginosa*. Another, from cowpats, is *Dendrobaena mammalis*. The way rooks shred the dried pats, sometimes worrying them to bits like a terrier with a rat, is a model of quiet efficiency. Other key food items, the choice of which has earned the rook praise from farmers for centuries, are the larval stage of several beetles, notably the cockchafer and also various members of the *Tipulidae* family, commonly known as daddy-longlegs or crane flies. Their grey maggot-like grubs are familiar to us as leatherjackets and still have the potential to be major agricultural pests.

The rook's adaptation to feed in open grassland habitats free of the choking cover of trees means that, like myself, the species is almost certainly an incomer to the Yare valley. The original home was probably somewhere on the open plains of Eurasia, and rooks are still more Asian than European in their distribution. They occupy vast swathes of the Mongolian and Manchurian grasslands, right through to the outskirts of Beijing and the shores of the Yellow Sea. To the west they've conquered the immense oceanic expanses of Russian and Asian grassland from about 160°E to a point half a world away on the Baltic coast.

Throughout much of this massive range, which probably represents in the region of 20 million square kilometres, largely in a 20-degree latitudinal belt between the fortieth and sixtieth meridians, the rook is represented by just two distinct races. The nominate form, the type which occurs in the UK, is found as far east as north-west Altai in Kazakhstan and China's northwest Sinkiang province. The birds of far eastern Siberia, Japan, Korea and east China form a separate race or subspecies (called *pastinator*) and are marginally different, with a much more restricted area of bare skin on the face.

As a consequence of their origins, rooks inhabit for me a secondary but similarly vast imaginative space. They open those dark eloquent wings like a great story book, conjuring the steppe landscapes and their numberless human hordes trekking forever westwards — the Cimmerians, the Scythians, Samatians, Alans, Huns, Magyars, Bulgars and Mongols. Mingled with the rolling *craa* notes is the sound of horsemen and their stocky short-legged ponies straining against the chafe of leather on sweat. Somewhere in the dark-brown iris of a rook is the faintest trace of its ancient journey out of inner Asia.

In western Europe the unbroken wildwood of the early Holocene, which developed with the retreat of the last ice sheets, would have been an impenetrable thicket to an invading bird of the open landscape. Rooks were dependent upon the westward spread of stock grazing and cereal agriculture from their original Middle Eastern settings to make their own entry into Europe. So when you next pass a rookery remember to stop and listen. Among the spring-summoning cacophony you'll hear the faintest echo of a Neolithic axe.

Even now those European countries with extensive forest cover are largely rook-free zones. In Scandinavia, for instance, there are only small pockets of breeding birds in the southernmost Baltic areas, while large parts of Germany have no rooks. In recent times the species has spread in France, but it is still largely absent from the southern half of the country. Closer to the Mediterranean rooks run up against an ecological barrier that excludes them almost as completely as the closed forest canopies of Scandinavia.

The birds need moisture-softened earth to probe for invertebrates, and the lack of precipitation in the south restricts their *Zirkeln* feeding technique. The birds of the central Anatolian plateau in Turkey are the most southerly populations in the European half of the rook's range (in China they extend almost into the tropics at about 30 degrees north, in northern Szechwan province). The rain which falls in the Mediterranean winter allows the birds to pass the non-breeding season in various southern European areas, but the species doesn't stay to breed in what might otherwise be highly suitable country, such as the extensive grass steppe areas of central Spain.

There are however two notable Mediterranean anomalies to this general pattern. The first is a pinprick of colour on the rook's European range map signalling a small cluster of rookeries in northern Spain. The isolated population of a few thousand pairs was discovered only in the 1950s around the city of León. The surrounding landscape is an extensive agricultural plain that lies on the edge of one of the highest rainfall zones in all Spain, conditions well suited to the species. Yet the birds around León are the most south-westerly breeding rooks in the world, whose nearest neighbours are more than 700 kilometres away in central France.

In 2004 I went with my friend Tim Dee to try to discover whether the Spanish population was a recently established colony derived from the regular winter influx of northern European birds. Perhaps some of these had remained to nest when they located the correct conditions in this one small enclave. Another possibility is that they represent a relict Hispanic population of ancient standing, that had once been more widely spread and had slowly contracted to the present vestige.

At the time of our visit the whole area was locked in the vice of a sudden cold snap. On local television the Spanish weatherman was cocooned in a woollen coat and huddled against the chart depicting this climatic anomaly. Perhaps it was the intense freeze, but León's agricultural hinterland seemed a melancholic place, where the mud-brick walls of the deserted villages were dissolving steadily back into the earth from which they'd once been raised. It felt like a forlorn Soviet experiment abandoned on the steppes of the USSR.

Then, unexpectedly, we struck gold. First we came across a tiny mud-brick village called Grajalejo — 'rooky place' — and later that same day we stumbled into Grajal — 'rookery' — a hamlet of perhaps a dozen buildings. They were ancient settlements whose occupants had named their villages after the most conspicuous noisy bird in the landscape, *el grajo*.

★ ★ ★

The one other historical population in the Mediterranean that deserves mention and raises similar questions, was recorded by none other than Virgil. In Book One of his bucolic idyll, the *Georgics*, published in 30 BC, the great Roman poet offers the tenderest observations of the bird's breeding habits and makes reference to the weather lore associated with rooks for more than 2,000 years:

> Then rooks, the guttural talkers, three times or four repeat
> A clear cool note, and often up there in the treetop cradles
> Charmed by some unfamiliar sweet impulse we cannot guess at
> Gossip among the leaves: they love, when rain is over,
> To visit again their baby brood, their darling nests.

It's not, to my belief, that God has given them
A special instinct, or Fate a wider fore-knowledge of things;
But, when the weather's changing, when the wet atmosphere
Shifts and a sky dripping from the south wind condenses
What was rare just now and rarefies what was condensed,
New images possess their mind, impulses move
Their heart other than moved them while the wind was herding the clouds.
Thus, the countryside over, begins that bird-chorale,
Beasts rejoice, and rooks caw in their exultation.

Virgil had clearly observed nesting rooks closely and had most probably seen them around his home town near Mantua, in the Po valley. Yet today it is impossible to hear the guttural talkers at their nests anywhere in Italy and the nearest breeding birds are in Switzerland or Slovenia. They may have retreated over the Alps because of climatic changes in northern Italy, or possibly because they were over-harvested to supply an Italian love of crow pie. But whatever the reason, rooks are now just winter visitors to the Italian peninsula.

* * *

Free of long snow cover in winter, with limited areas of forest and swept by warm moisture-laden maritime weather systems, Britain is in a wholly different category for rooks to almost any other country in Europe. Only Belarus currently boasts a population of comparable size. The last census suggested nearly a million pairs and my hunch is that they are now far more numerous. The United Kingdom and Ireland combined have almost 40 per cent of the entire rook population in Europe. Even in the Yare valley there are more rooks than breed in Austria, or the Czech Republic, Finland, Norway, Spain or Switzerland.

An attachment to farmland is still fundamental to the bird's British distribution and it's telling that the largest area where rooks are absent today is beyond the Great Glen in northern Scotland, where agriculture is at its most marginal. Yet wherever we've replaced trees with grassland or arable, even in the chemical-drenched monocultures of the twenty-first century, rooks make a healthy living. To thrive, however, they require at least some trees, invariably tall trees, which are the preferred nest location throughout the entire transcontinental range.

Occasionally a pair has been known to exchange the canopy's wind-tossed cradle for a nest on the ground. In historic times rooks have also been recorded as taking up temporary residence on church steeples and other similar man-made equivalents.

Recently at Shellhaven near Coryton on the north bank of the Thames in Essex there was a small colony of about thirty pairs nesting on the metal gangways surrounding an old gasometer owned by the Shell oil company. It may well be unique. Yet of the approximately 40,000 rook nests I've examined in the last few years, all have been in trees. No more than a handful have been lower than five metres.

Another limiting factor is the rook's dislike of high country. The 300-metre contour line places a rough cordon around them, excluding them from the highest of our upland spaces, but wherever the birds occur you'll find some combination of the two key elements — trees and fields — whether it's the patchwork plots and lichen-bearded elm breaks of the Cornish lanes; or the gaunt black sycamore stands in Derbyshire's dry-walled pasture; or the alder carr along the

Suffolk valley bottoms, the beech-topped chalk knolls of Hertfordshire, or the breast-soft folds of north Lancashire. Even in the eastern section of the Lake District you see rooks squeezed into available plantation cover among the sour green hills that climb towards Shap. In the East Anglian fens rooks occupy a landscape almost as open as their original steppe and to nest they crowd into the tall garden trees clustered around the ancient 'island' settlements of north Cambridgeshire.

During previous centuries the lingering rural character of our towns meant that rooks could sling their stick hammocks in the very heart of the largest cities. In Norwich they were once a distinctive feature of urban life. The seventeenth-century polymath Sir Thomas Browne wrote of the birds being harvested in the suburbs and put on sale in Norwich market, where their livers were prized as a cure for rickets.

An older London once had numerous rookeries. A famous long-lived example stood in the garden of the Temple, now on the Victoria Embankment. It was recorded at the time of the Great Fire in 1666 and was celebrated more than a century later by both Oliver Goldsmith and Charles Lamb. The windows in Goldsmith's residence overlooked the colony and he relished the clamorous hustle and wrote with loving inaccuracy of the birds' nuptial lives. The rookery vanished when Queen Victoria was still a girl, but at the other end of Chancery Lane the legal profession retained a thriving colony for almost another hundred years. However, creeping urban sprawl enforced on the rooks an ever greater journey to the nearest available fields. Eventually habitat loss defeated even their loyalty to metropolitan life and the last birds were gone by 1916.

In a sense the fate of the old London rookeries tells the story of the Yare valley birds in reverse. As the capital lost its open character and development buried the final agricultural nooks and crannies, so it lost the bird *par excellence* of cow pasture and arable plot. Today on a map of British rook distribution the Greater London area represents the only other cavity in an otherwise solid block of colour.

But along the Yare the river secured the rook's fortunes. The flood plain is so low lying and wet that few farmers have risked conversion to arable. It is still 90 per cent grassland and the triangular bloc lying between Yarmouth, Acle and Haddiscoe is the largest area of lowland grazing marsh in England. It is rook heaven.

By the time we moved to the valley in 2001

my own needs were aligned to the ecology of my sacred bird. I felt deeply jaded by the congested terraced streets of inner Norwich. I wanted to break free. I wanted an airborne cradle of sticks from which to scan the world passing below, wide horizons to stretch my gaze, and the open space with its faint breath of the steppe to fire my imagination.

9

It is part of the ritual of rooking in the Yare valley that I always carry four items during my spring visits. In one coat pocket I have my notebook and pen. In the other I have one of those mechanical counters used by train conductors, with a rotating face of numbers that increase with each click of the button. I use it for counting the nests in the trees.

When you're monitoring a site like the one near Reedham called Park Carr, a kilometre-long wood with over 500 pairs of birds, a counter is absolutely essential. It banishes the need for complicated mental arithmetic. My mind is free to focus on the footwork or any sort of brief distraction so that I can simply walk along, eyes on the trees, and click for every nest that I spot. It probably also ensures an element of objectivity. There may be a sneaky temptation to boost or reduce a rookery's total to accord with some precon-ceived theory. So I complete the census without ever looking at the counter, and I don't know the total until the last nest is logged.

In the same pocket as my counter is the

fourth item — a small piece of flint about the size of a rabbit's kidney, worn smooth by the action of water, crazed with a landscape of time-inflicted craters, grooves and scratches, immensely comfortable to the hand and black in colour like the rooks themselves. I found it at Burgh St Peter, near the River Waveney at the south-eastern extremity of my patch. As if to fix the spot in my memory, I have as a marker for its discovery the compelling silhouette of St Mary's Church.

The building is remarkable enough for being isolated on the edge of the marshes — it's at least three kilometres from the village of Burgh St Peter — but St Mary's has the strangest outline of any church in the region. Four rectangular brick lozenges rise in separate storeys over a wider plinth formed by the base of an original sixteenth-century tower. Each storey is smaller than the one below and the whole structure resembles a gigantic wedding cake; but apparently it was meant to echo the ziggurats of ancient Mesopotamia.

In a way this architectural folly reflects one of the reasons I carry the stone in the first place. My piece of flint is itself a kind of church — a small venerable contemplative space, a steel-hard, steel-cold touchstone reminding me that the residence of rooks and humans alike in this place is a thing of extreme transience. The birds have been here perhaps no more than 5,000 years and Neolithic farmers a little longer. The stone, however, which is hardly distinct from the countless other flints glinting across the fields of this landscape, is an immensely ancient treasure at least 70–90 million years old. It's on my desk as I type these words.

Flint like this is composed of re-deposited silica from the exoskeletons of marine creatures such as sponges and sea urchins. They lived once on the bed of a broad, warm tropical sea in the Upper Cretaceous and were contemporaries of those weird, paddle-limbed reptile giants known as ichthyosaurs and plesiosaurs. As the sea urchins died their deposits of silica drizzled on to the seabed, where they oozed or leached through faults in the accumulating sediments of chalk. Over millions of years they metamorphosed into continuous beds of 'tabular' or scattered pieces of 'nodule' flint.

The small kidney-shaped fragment in my pocket is a stone originating from the sea. It is a bit of land created of water and here's the central importance of my flint, because so too is the Yare valley, particularly Halvergate and Haddiscoe Island. This stone is a distillation both of the sea, and of the processes of change that can convert water into Halver-gate. In a sense I have with me the whole history of the landscape in my pocket.

★　★　★

My flint could have reached Burgh St Peter in one of several ways: bulldozed here by the ice during any of several glaciations, or swept downstream off a Jurassic plateau in the English Midlands by ancient rivers once flowing east as tributaries of the Rhine. Whatever the method of transfer, I cherish the idea that it was a wave-washed pebble on a long-vanished beach and that it lay on that spot as the valley evolved from enclosed sea to open marsh and then to terra firma, until the day I rescued it from oblivion. This much is incontrovertible. The place at which I found it is exactly the point where the sea would have lapped against the shore.

From that strand line there is a shallow rise southwards on to what would have been a narrow tongue of 'upland' projecting east into an island-rimmed section of the North Sea. A little over 2,000 years ago an Iron Age farmer would have stood on the crown of this coastal headland with salt water visible on three sides. Ahead of him, to the east, across a broad channel, would have been the low-lying island of Lothingland (modernday Lowestoft stands on this ancient shoal). All along the southern edge of the narrow isthmus was an arm of the sea inlet while, to the north and north-east, as far the eye could see, where Haddiscoe Island and Halvergate Marshes now stand, was another, this part a huge expanse of water.

⋆   ⋆   ⋆

Over the period of Halvergate's slow transition from water to land the place continued to yield the fundamental products of the open sea. Norwich and Beccles, the settlements at the opposite ends of the two twisting sea arms, were once important ports for herring, which were partly caught on the saline estuaries that flowed all the way to the outskirts of each town. Beccles alone paid an annual toll in Saxon times of 30,000 herring, which William the Conqueror doubled after his assessors had finished their Domesday inventory.

Throughout the whole of the Middle Ages the Yare was a watery world yielding a prodigious harvest. The locals used huge buskin or bushing nets that were 30 yards long (27 metres) set along the edges of the reeds for coarse fish. Even as late as the nineteenth century a fisherman declared: 'We thought nothing of catching a ton of roach and bream in a day, in the Beccles or Norwich rivers (the Waveney or the Yare); and we often put back three parts of our catch because we could not sell so much.' The fish were often so superfluous to requirements that they were used to manure the Yare's adjacent fields.

Eventually the scale of the catch started to impact upon stock, but an inquiry into the management of Broadland fisheries drew the following testimony from one old poacher. At spawning grounds near Surlingham, the huge numbers of fish were such 'that it seemed as if a boat could hardly be rowed among them. On a fine hot day the backs of the huge bream could be seen breaking the surface in every direction; and in the stillness of the night the splashing and suckings and wallowings, the shakings of the reeds as the monsters rolled through them . . . were striking in the extreme.' Another remarked that on a moonlit night the broad surface reminded him of a 'Stilton cheese all alive with maggots'.

For centuries eels also snaked into another set of bulging nets. During the Elizabethan period there were thirty-eight eel-stations in the Broads that fishermen could rent and operate for a whole year. One at Hardley Cross, just downstream from our house, marked the boundary between the civic jurisdictions of Great Yarmouth and Norwich. From the 'uplands' just south of the spot is a great panorama of the whole valley which only Burgh Castle can rival. But by the river itself, at Hardley Cross there was an eel-sett in the mid-nineteenth century where over four nights just under two tonnes of eels were caught.

These fish harvests declined in close proportion to the intensifying human grip on the river, the marsh and the estuary. As the Yare became more land than water, so the eels and other aquatic life vanished. By the end of the nineteenth century 40 stones (250 kilos) of eels was a remarkably good catch and a satisfactory session might produce just 10–15 stone (60–90 kilos). In 2004, setts for eels were manned in the Broads that produced not a single sinuous fish.

★   ★   ★

The declining fisheries, both fresh and salt, were a good measure of the valley's transformation from water to land, but the process of conversion dated right back to the Romans. They knew the land-cleaving channel of salt water as Gariensis. Towards the end of empire, as they came under threat from Saxon pirates, they built two great forts to guard the estuary's open jaws from maritime invasion. The remains of one are in the coastal town of Caistor St Edmund, but it once stood on an island known subsequently as Flegg (the Old Norse for 'flat'). A twin called Garionnonum lay across the channel on the northern edge of the neighbouring island of Lothingland. Familiar today as Burgh Castle, it is the largest Roman structure surviving in Norfolk — the huge walls still run for hundreds of metres — and Roman triremes once sailed through Gariensis and rode at anchor beneath its ramparts. Today that same anchorage is 11 kilometres from the open sea. Yet it is a measure of the Romans' sense of strategic location that the fort still commands the best possible views over Halvergate and Haddiscoe.

As you look out from Burgh Castle the whole panoramic expanse before you looks and feels like a sea of grass. In a sense, that's what it is. Today it forms the largest surviving area of lowland grazing marsh in Britain, whose fame dates back at least three centuries. In 1721, in his *Tour Through England and Wales*, Daniel Defoe described how the Yare flowed through 'a long tract of the richest meadows, and the largest, take them all together, that are anywhere in England'. The Romans initiated the process of embankment that steadily converted it from water to dry land, but the Saxons consolidated a policy of internal colonisation, wresting fresh pasture from what was once open estuary or saltmarsh.

By the time of Domesday, Halvergate and Haddiscoe were listed for their large flocks of sheep, and I can already hear the rooks' hoarse *craa* notes mingled with the tinkle of bells, the barking dogs, the rough voices of the shepherds enfolding their flocks; I can see the jackdaws in spring plucking wool straight off the backs of the sheep, and rooks tearing the dung apart in their search for fresh grubs to stab down the blood-coloured craws of a squalling brood.

During the high Middle Ages sheep retained their dominance in the Yare but by the sixteenth century cattle had begun to replace them. The reticulated pattern of dyke-segmented pasture, visible on Halvergate and Haddiscoe today, was already established by the early eighteenth century. Defoe described the annual cattle drives bringing as many as 40,000 head across half of Britain, some from as far away as Ireland or the Isle of Skye, to a market just north of Norwich. He wrote: 'These Scots 'runts' as they call them coming out of the cold and barren mountains of the Highlands of Scotland, feed so eagerly on the rich pasture of its marshes that they thus in unusual manner grow monstrously fat, and the beef is so delicious for taste that the inhabitants prefer them to the English cattle.'

★   ★   ★

For all its history as terra firma, the sense of Haddiscoe and Halvergate as a stretch of open water remains imprinted on my imagination, as if a ghost image of the sea lay just below the physical features. Haddiscoe also retains one of the sea's fundamental qualities. It's a landscape that yields very little sense of its age. It's very hard to think of the sea as old. The restless motion makes it appear constantly renewed. It's a medium that seems to have no past. It's just there, in an endless present.

It makes me think that in order to project a sense of the past upon a geographical place the human imagination requires something three dimensional, some relief, on which to frame it. Think of mountains. Their monumental scale is permeated with a sense of age and of the past. They dwarf us both physically and chronologically, looming behind and beyond us. We have the impression that they will always be there. That sacred stillness of mountains is surely one reason why journeys to and from them form an intrinsic element of most religions.

But flat landscapes, like open water, resist the processes of memory. They seem too plain, too ordinary to have acquired a history. Perhaps it's one more reason why we feel we can desecrate them with impunity. It's certainly one more reason why I keep my black flint pebble in my pocket. It reminds me to show reverence towards this wonderful place, to give thanks for its spare features, its simple line, its open skies and its emptiness.

In one more strange and unexpected way the rooks compound my thalassic impressions at Haddiscoe. True, they're among the most terrestrial of birds, with origins in Asia, one of the most landlocked places on Earth. Yet here in the Yare valley their rookeries are clustered on the geological timeline where I found my pebble, on the relic shores of the old vanished Gariensis. The grassland itself, which is the precise reason the birds are here, has replaced the open water. In order to be closest to it, the birds have built their nests, possibly for 2,000 years, at the point where the land finally tilts up off the flats into the 'uplands'. In effect they're breeding on the beach.

Their behaviour speaks of deeper ecological parallels between the open water and open grass. In the nesting season, the abundant supply of worms is the key to the rook's success. The onset of the breeding cycle in earliest spring is timed to coincide with the maximum availability of prey for the chicks. But the food items aren't spread evenly beneath the surface of the grass, they're clustered randomly. The unpredictability of locating this scattered food is proposed by ecologists as a reason for the bird's colonial lifestyle. It's thought that rooks have evolved to share resources and capitalise on the shifting and temporary abundances by pursuing a feeding strategy of follow-my-leader.

Spring brings its typical scenario. A rook that finds a rich spot harvests the worms and leatherjackets until a sublingual extension in the mouth, known as the bucchal pouch, is bulging and can hold no more. After it has flown back to the rookery to deposit the highly visible catch with partner or chicks, the same bird will then automatically return to the site of its easy pickings and draw with it any adult rooks that are foraging less successfully. Each bird discovering a food hotspot faces the disadvantage of competition from neighbours, but it is more than compensated by the opportunity, on all occasions when it's less successful, to share the good fortune uncovered by others.

An unpredictable food source requires other adaptations. Rooks nest within a brief time window, so that all the young emerge together and their parents must gather food at the same moment. Their collective foraging ensures efficiency in locating that unseen and randomly concentrated supply. Rooks have an inbuilt insurance to accommodate seasons of poor foraging. Their eggs are incubated not after the last one is laid, but usually after the second has appeared. Technically it's known as asynchronous incubation. It means that the young hatching from eggs laid after the second will be less developed, while the first-born chicks have had time to build up strength. In times of hardship the larger young will acquire the lion's share of the meagre food supply, but they may well survive when their smaller siblings do not. Nature is ruthlessly efficient.

All of these characteristics — communal nest sites, simultaneous breeding, collective foraging and asynchronous incubation and hatching — are behaviour patterns shared by many types of seabird, precisely because they face the same challenge of a highly unpredictable food source. But while all these seabirds fly offshore to hunt for unseen prey beneath the water's surface, the rooks are fishing in the earth.

As I park the car near Crab Apple Lane and wander down to the rookery — my favourite — in the alder carr behind Thorpe Hall, on the edge of Thorpe Marshes, I can watch the constant passage of adult rooks away from their nests on the old beach, out to the expanse of grassland to the north. I rotate the black flint pebble in my pocket and the whole place resolves into two elements: the black birds fishing across a sea of green. Then out of that hazy vastness they come rowing back to shore with the promise of new life bulked in their throats.

10

'But why rooks?' my mother pleaded when
she first heard about my obsession with them.
For more than thirty years she's maintained
her benign maternal gaze upon my ornithological passion, but her face acquired an
unfamiliar quizzical look whenever we spoke
of rooks, as if she was overwhelmed by their
ordinariness. The thing that surprised her
most was my love of the bird's voice. Her
expression seemed to demand to know how
much pleasure could be gained from a crude,
toneless monosyllable.

The term we've overused to describe the
sound of a rook is 'caw'. It is a word that does
convey something of the simpler, less varying
cry of the carrion crow. Although the sound
of the rook may be coarser, as if the air
flowing through the bird's syrinx passes over
something immensely rough, far less effort
actually goes into its production. But the
hard, gnarled, shrunken note of a carrion
crow seems the result of a force that comes
close to pain.

'Caw' may capture very little of the rook's
vocal repertoire but the onomatopoeic name

itself, rook, is just as unsatisfactory. Better than either is the original Anglo-Saxon version *broc*, which suggests something of the adenoidal timbre and the rolled *rrs* locked into the middle portion of the syllable. Best of all as a transliteration of the call is the vernacular Scottish name, 'Craa', which nicely captures its drawn-out quality as well as the gravelliness.

A key element that distinguishes rook sounds from those of the carrion crow flows from the rook's communal lifestyle. Their calls are given their depth and complexity by the constant recession of echoes and responses from neighbours. It means that they have a conversational informality and ease. Even in the dead of night, many hours after the roost has assembled at Buckenham Carrs, I've heard the birds keep up a comfort blanket of sounds. Their whole lives, from stick cradle to grave, are robed in a flowing, gurgling current of music.

Over the last few years, in the course of conversation with dozens of people, I've conducted a straw poll on the rook's voice and found that almost all are in favour. Most revealing was an old boy I stopped near the rookery at Postwick. We shouldn't really like it, he suggested, because on the face of it, it is an unattractive sound, but somehow he still enjoyed it. It made him think of his childhood on the Isle of Man. Rooks have the gift to remind us, it seems, of who we once were.

Not everyone loves them. Thomas Carlyle once suggested that to hold a dialogue with a rookery was the most complete image of chaos he could imagine. Shortly after I'd acquired the rook habit I heard the story of a man called before the courts in Edinburgh for trying to exterminate a rookery. The racket was driving him mad. I think he and Carlyle are in a minority simply because most people don't really hear the calls of rooks in the ordinary sense. The sound may register in a subliminal way but seldom breaks through to a person's listening ear. It's the life of these calls beyond our conscious mind which helps me to explain the near-ubiquitous use of rook vocalisations in television and radio.

Test it. You'll find it almost impossible to see or hear a programme with a rural setting and *not* have rooks calling in the distance. It is especially the case when the programme-maker wishes to denote a switch of scene from city to countryside. Rooks are the classic shorthand for that change of setting. In many ways they are the obvious choice. In Britain rook calls are free of most geographical and seasonal limitations in a way that conventional birdsong, or owl hoots, or other country noises are not. My guess is that even the sound engineers and producers themselves are not really aware of the rook's versatility in this regard. Nor do they choose the rook in a deliberate, premeditated way. At the appropriate part in their drama they simply sample a disk marked 'Country Sounds' and out of our rural unconscious flies the flock of raucous birds, without anyone giving them a second thought.

The bird's universal presence on television and radio also demonstrates to me how deeply embedded it is in our notion of the British countryside. I think it is this seamless identification of the calls with the natural environment that is the basal note in my own enjoyment of them. Quite simply, rook sounds are our landscape, particularly the English landscape, made audible. The point is all the better made by a poet from Scotland, Andrew Young, in 'The Farmer's Gun':

The wood is full of rooks
That by their faded looks
No more on thievery will thrive,
As when they were alive,
Nor fill the air with the hoarse noise
That most of all is England's pleasant voice.

A key revelation as our relationship evolved was that the harsh notes are only the commonest element in the rook's songbook. Gradually my ears began to pick out the full complement of calls, and to detect an emotional register behind the variation. If you can manage to get close to a rookery without disturbing the occupants you realise that in these quieter moments their typical *craa* notes are flatter and more even in quality, suggesting the birds' emotional neutrality. When they are at their most relaxed and meditative I've heard calls that are mingled with a soft chicken-like *chooking* sound. The great Scottish naturalist of the nineteenth century, William Macgillivray, once visited a rookery under cover of darkness and wrote of 'the soft clear modulated notes' and the 'fondling and coaxing calls' used by mother birds towards their offspring.

Another great student of the rook was Edmund Selous, younger brother of Frederick, the famous African game-hunter and travel writer. Selous junior returned to the species in three of his books and claimed to recognise thirty different calls, which I can well believe. His noble attempts at transliteration — for example 'Chack-a, chack-a', or 'How-chow', or 'Hook-a-hoo-loo' — were honestly intended but almost impossible to cross-reference with my own field experience. Few rook calls commend themselves to our ears as human syllables and yet, like many of the corvid family, rooks can become expert talkers when kept in captivity. Macgillivray knew of a pet bird that could even imitate the barking of various dogs in the West Lothian village of Bathgate.

One pleasure I've yet to experience is the sound of rooks singing. It is not particularly unusual. Gilbert White heard it more than two centuries ago, but he remained unimpressed by the performance. 'Rooks, in the breeding season, attempt sometimes in the gaiety of their hearts to sing,' he wrote in a letter to Daines Barrington, 'but with no great success.' Yet in his book *Crows of the World*, my friend, the great corvophile Derek Goodwin, was more appreciative:

The song consists of a medley of much or all of the Rook's repertoire, usually given rather more softly than in other contexts. Various soft cawing, gurgling, rattling and crackling calls are uttered and the general effect is very much like that of a singing Starling, only louder . . . In late winter, in 1946 in northern Yorkshire, a sudden thaw after about a week of frost and heavy snow cover set a great many Rooks singing. I saw and heard many individual Rooks singing in the sun, although the snow had not at the moment melted sufficiently to bare the soil and so it was unlikely that they had fed better than during the previous days.

The context of all these strange warbling rooks suggests that inner contentment is integral to the performance. Yet it is more usual to encounter the birds when they're in a state of anxiety, partly because they are so nervous of humans, but also, like many highly social animals, they seem to enjoy a permanent background excitability. As the mood rises you can detect more intense elements gathering in the voice. A frequent indicator of alarm when you approach a rookery in the breeding season is the presence of an inflected rise after the opening portion of the *craa* note. When they are really excited the pitch ascends to a gull-like wailing or yelping that has the same delicious ambivalence as the gull's cry, a blend of hysteria with delight.

A call which I can't help trying to express in human terms is a note I describe as 'brilling'. I think Selous must have heard it when he wrote of a 'burring note, which, though much deeper and essentially rook-like in tone, at once reminded me of the well-known sound made by the nightjar. Imagine a rook trying to 'burr' or 'churr' like a nightjar, and doing it like a rook, and you have it.' To me it resembles a child pursing their lips and blowing hard to vibrate them as if trying to imitate the noise of an engine. I can hardly hear a rook doing it without it bringing to mind the image of a young boy racing along and making the same sound as he rattles his stick down the park railings.

Rooks calling together in particularly large congregations, such as at their winter roost, can evoke a suite of collective human parallels: the shapeless hum of distant traffic or the emotional rise and fall of a football crowd. Should anything excite them further at the moment of take-off — a gun's discharge or a low-flying jet — the sporting analogy becomes even more appropriate, because the roar rises in pitch and volume just as if the home team had grabbed a late winner.

Very occasionally I can hear sounds that resemble an individual human voice. The godfather of soul, James Brown, interspersed the song's lyrics with climactic shrieks and whoops that fall well within the range of rook vocalisations. And another specific human analogy is the hard, rasping, animal sound we make when in the throes of exertion . . . or ecstasy. What, I ask any critic of the rook's voice, could be more joyful or life-affirming than that?

Part of the enormous pleasure of all the sounds is the context. They are at their most expressive and beautiful around the period of the two solstices — winter and summer. At the dead moments of the year, when almost everything in nature is silent, they seem to acquire an added vibrancy and passion, the whole winter landscape acting like a great resonating chamber to amplify their power.

Strangely, perhaps, the impact is almost as strong in late summer. By July the Yare valley rooks start to gather in a shortlived roost on my side of the river in a wood called Mulberry Carr. They use it for just three or four months before resuming a relationship with their usual night harbour on the other side at Buckenham. For that period the flock is within earshot of the house and whenever I walk down the lane to watch them their sounds come at me with subtle echoes and resonances as if from a great cavernous space. It is one of the curious paradoxes of summer. It's the time of year when life has reached the point of maximum expansion. Yet summer seems to suck down its own strength, hollowing itself out from the inside, and there is a strange but wonderful silence and stillness within it.

Often, as dusk falls, the only other sound in this entire summer landscape, aside from the corvids, is that of playing children, their cries modulating with the emotional tempo of their game. Distance reduces it to simple inarticulate noise, which makes them seem just one more wild inhabitant in their native habitat. Even after nightfall the roosting birds keep up a constant babble and on warm balmy summer evenings it's often the first sound to greet me as I climb out of the car after a day away working in London. I am entered by those sounds in the darkness and I cannot tell you how good it feels. The mental detritus of the city is sluiced away instantly and I am reconnected with the place and my true self. No other wild animal, nothing in the natural world, can do that for me in the same way.

★   ★   ★

Whatever the time of year, rooks are unfailingly accompanied by jackdaws and if I'm honest I love the sound of that species even more. Both syllables in its common name are onomatopoeic. The *daw* part echoes a drawn-out hoarse note not too dissimilar to the rook's own, although it is usually higher and reedier in quality. The more common sound is the *jack*, a sharp crisp lapidary call which resembles two flawless pieces of flint being rapped smartly together. Jackdaws are intensely vocal and when gathered *en masse* sustain contact notes almost irrespective of the hour or their background activity.

When flocking with rooks they are almost always the dominant sound partner regardless of their number, a point observed long ago by the Victorian Richard Jefferies. 'As the black multitude floats past overhead with deliberate easy flight,' he wrote in *Wild Life in a Southern Country*, 'their trumpeters and buglemen, the jackdaws — two or three to every company — utter their curious chuckle; for the jackdaw is a bird which could not keep silence to save his life, but must talk after his fashion, while his grave, solemn companions move slowly onwards, rarely deigning to 'caw' him a reply.' Jackdaws in flight have a habit of answering their neighbours so that the explosive calls from one bird will detonate near-instantaneous responses, the sounds ricocheting back and forth through the flock in a slow-dying wave.

On an occasion when I went to watch an exceptional corvid roost in Anglesey, which included one of the largest gatherings of ravens ever recorded in the world, the tonal contrast was between jackdaw and raven, rather than rook and jackdaw. The effect was deeply impressive. Ravens produce a guttural croak beyond the human vocal range, with perhaps the exception of that fabulous unworldly throat-singing of Tibetan Buddhist monks. As they came barrelling through the trees to the roost, the ravens unleashed sounds that seemed as if they were just unlocked from a block of granite, or from deep down within a primeval bog. Yet when the jackdaws swooped into the same trees they produced a sudden impulsive flush of calls like a refreshing rain shower. Thereafter every single jackdaw recruit triggered a fresh ricochet of joy notes. The difference between the sounds of the two close relatives could not have been greater.

These calls create around jackdaws an invincible aura of cheerfulness that once gave rise to a deliciously comic moment I witnessed at a roost near the hamlet of Thorpe in the lower Yare valley. A flock of about 2,000 corvids made up largely of jackdaws had just rained down by moonlight into the canopy of their roost trees amid an ecstasy of *jakking* sounds. Way below, almost from the shrub layer, came the slow, sad hoot of a solitary tawny owl. It gave the distinct impression of feeling very nervous in the presence of so many potentially hostile corvids. Yet one sensed that it just had to call out, simply to cloak itself in its own melancholy music against the tide of infectious merriment all around.

A striking aspect of jackdaw calls is that they produce a surprisingly harmonious interplay with the sounds of rooks. The high crisp timbre is so distinct from the other bird's voice that one wonders if, during their millennia of companionship, the two birds have evolved voices that complement instead of interfering with each other's intra-specific communications. Elsewhere I have described the metallic notes of jackdaws as 'seeming like sharp fragments embedded in the more continuous, deep, shovelling-gravel roar of the rooks.' Jackdaw calls are shards of flint in a rook earth, brilliant sparks of light in the wider darkness of rook music.

When flight lines of both species pass overhead on their way to the roost their joint vocalisations invoke, for me, the flow of water, not necessarily for their direct resemblance to the noise of a stream, but because they are stream-like in their ceaseless, random structure, and in their capacity to soothe and mesmerise the senses. Eventually out of the larger current of notes emerge striking oddities — the pleading of a lost kitten, a metallic *twong* like a stone skimming across thick ice, the initial hoarse gulp of mating marsh frogs *Rana ridibunda*, a curious oboe-like note heard just once, the nasal *scaarp*, alarm call of common snipe, the neurotic *brrrrrruk* of a fleeing moorhen; one rarity I particularly enjoy is the rook's *craa* call delivered in super-slow time so that it resembles the reluctant movement of a very rusty gate, a hard granule of sound for each degree of swing.

In the winter of 2004–2005 the Buckenham roost had eventually swollen by late January to around 40,000 birds, the largest it has been in my years of watching. It created a music that I count among the most wonderful produced by anything I've heard in the realms of nature. It was at its most compelling when the birds launched into the air in their final flight to the roost. Just as I no longer viewed the vibrant mushroom cloud of black spiralling above the woods as a flock of rooks and jackdaws, so I ceased to hear their voices as those of birds. It was an elemental clamour and I found myself making the hour's return journey round the Yare to Buckenham Carrs simply to hear it at full volume one more time.

On one occasion I was fortunate to have

with me my friend, the BBC radio producer, Tim Dee. Together we were making a series of programmes on the life of the rook throughout the year. On that evening I didn't so much hear the birds; the highlight was the sense of confirmation in the look on Tim's face. 'Wonderful,' he kept repeating, 'wonderful.' They came at us in a single dark outpouring when the individual calls of the rooks and jackdaws melted into an all-consuming torrent. I seemed to be hearing a sound produced before the fundamental elements of life — silicon, carbon, oxygen, hydrogen — had been broken down, redistributed and composed into 10 million species. It had an irresistible quality like the gravitational pull of the moon, luminous like the roar of stars, an oceanic up-current that engulfed a flood plain and changed my life for ever.

11

Whenever I reach for the boots and binoculars and head out of the door I could go in any direction from the house to find wildlife. Yet something hard-wired in my brain means that the internal compass always trends to the River Yare, or some offspring body of water that eventually makes its sluggish meandering course back into the parent further downstream. The Yare is my lodestone in this landscape and I sometimes wonder what it is about the water that draws me back each time.

The answer may well lie buried about three metres beneath my neighbours' garden. Several years ago they found a mysterious hard object in the deep, soft, black, peaty soil of one of their fields. After several days' excavation, latterly with a small mechanical digger, they unearthed what local archaeologists believed to be the remains of a Neolithic or Bronze Age boat.

Stone Age people were almost certainly drawn to this place, which was then right on the edge of the great tidal estuary of Gariensis. They were in search of what ecologists call ecotones, contact zones between distinct habitats. Coastal strips and river banks, the margins of tidal creeks and marshy areas between terra firma and the open water are classic examples. They were attractive to our ancestors because they are often the richest points in any landscape for wildlife. Just as Neolithic foragers were disposed to paddle along these borders, the modern naturalist is ineluctably drawn to the same space. Although I'm foraging for words and they sought edible plants, shells, fish and fowl, both of us make the same intrinsic hunter-gatherer's choice. Margins are best.

The boat in next door's field confirms that the Yare valley has long been a bird landscape, and it reminds me that I'm not the first hunter-gatherer to make a living from it. I find the few glimpses we have of these older bird people both tantalising and deeply instructive. They give me a sense of community that overarches time. I have often met fellow naturalists in far-flung parts of the world. Our rapport is instantaneous, regardless of geographical distance or language barrier. My guess is that a shared passion for observing species other than our own would transcend the centuries just as easily.

Carl Jung suggested that 'There are people who, psychologically, might be living in the year 5000 BC, i.e., who can still successfully solve their conflicts as people did seven thousand years ago. There are countless troglodytes and barbarians living in Europe and in all civilized countries.' I count myself among the barbarians. I wonder if some of the mental make-up of any naturalist is inherited directly from Neolithic forebears. We fulfil ourselves as they did, resolving some of the problems of modern life as they might.

I'd love to spend time with these birdmen of the past, especially the people who built the boat next door. One question I'd ask is whether they saw their own past reflected back at them through the landscape. In any physical space today we come up against the legacy of history all the time. The dykes, the hedges, the fields are full of memories of the old hands which made them, just as the barbed-wire fences and no-entry signs bring us up against its political past. We imagine because these ancient ancestors lived, so to speak, before our own 'past' had even happened, that they came to it untrammelled by filters or restraints or preconceptions. They saw it as it was, as in a first dawn.

Yet perhaps they too found the landscape steeped in familial memories, rich in their own ancestors' oral tales, which were passed down round the camp-fire generation to generation. No matter what the age, we all feel — we relish it, perhaps, like a great enveloping overcoat — the great weight of history in a landscape, and sense ourselves to be at the end of a long process.

Another thing I'd want to know is what wildlife was here in the Neolithic era. The very best I can do is go back a mere thirty-five generations, which is wonderful enough. I can go back because William Haward, William de Hanyngfeld and William de Sutton were brought together in the reign of Edward I to form a commission of inquiry 'touching the persons who entered the park of Hugh de Bardolf . . . and . . . carried away his eyries of sparrow-hawks, herons, spoon-bills and bitterns in his several woods'. Two of the places where the three Williams investi-gated the robbing of birds' nests were Cantley and Strumpshaw, villages just over the river from where we now live.

The document is dated 22 March 1300 and is the first written evidence I am aware of about the bird populations in the Yare valley. It therefore opens a priceless vista on to the landscape of 700 years ago. Spoonbills, those striking white water birds of heron-like shape and size, have the singular quirk of a laterally flattened spatulate bill. To feed they sweep this bizarre appendage through the water, where it acts like a fine-meshed sieve trapping aquatic prey. For hundreds of years spoonbills were no more than irregular visitors to Britain in small numbers, but just recently they have recovered a precarious toehold as a nesting species. In 1999 a pair raised two young in north-west England, becoming the first successful breeding spoonbills in Britain in more than three centuries.

During the time of William Haward and his friends, however, spoonbills were widespread and the Yare valley was a stronghold.

The precise reason the birds crept marginally into the human record is that the young were captured and penned to be fattened and eaten. Spoonbills were highly valued as food.

More than 350 years after the three Williams' inquiry into the Bardolf estates, the Norwich scholar Sir Thomas Browne described the enduring presence of spoonbills in the Yare valley. Browne must have seen them nesting in woods bordering the great sweep of river where it finally tilts north towards Yarmouth. He used a lost English name for the bird, 'the platea or shouelard,' and noted that 'they build upon the tops of high trees. [T]hey haue [sic] formerly built in the Hernerie at Claxton & Reedham.' His implication that they had abandoned the region in the recent past makes the seventeenth-century scholar one of the final witnesses to this lost ornithological spectacle.

I can't make much of these few sentences alone. Browne gave no further clues to the spoonbills' life in the Yare valley, save to tell us that they were shot for their plumage rather than their flesh. The one item in his account on which we can build much more is his reference to the 'Hernerie' at Reedham. Grey herons were a surviving fixture in the woods adjacent to the village and were repeatedly observed until the early twentieth century, when there were as many as ninety nesting pairs. Herons may thus have bred in the same spot, where the spoonbills were once noted, for a thousand years.

In Sir Thomas Browne's youth the site at Reedham was clearly a combined colony of the two species. But the scholar's observations acquire their full significance alongside another incidental reference. He noted elsewhere in the same book, *Notes and Letters on the Natural History of Norfolk*, that the spoonbills and herons shared the nest trees with a third large fish-eating species, the cormorant. In fact this Reedham population was so well known that its fame had reached the King's ear. James I was a keen fisherman and experimented with various offbeat techniques, including the use of ospreys and otters to catch fish for him. These charismatic anglers clearly proved less reliable than the humble cormorant, because while they vanished from the royal records, James took to keeping the great black water birds at Westminster, and fishing with them became a Stuart pastime for decades. We know his son maintained the tradition because in his book Sir Thomas Browne wrote of the cormorants 'building at Reedham upon trees from whence King Charles the first was wont to bee supplied'.

The snapshot offered by the Bardolf inquiry of 1300, in combination with Browne's description from the seventeenth century, starts to build a far richer scene. The two accounts imply that throughout the Middle Ages, heron, spoonbill and cormorant shared, in some combination, their nesting places at the floodplain margin at Strump-shaw, Cantley, Claxton and Reedham. Today there's not a single site in Britain where cormorants, herons and spoonbills all nest together. To witness a comparable tableau you'd have to travel to some of the last great wetlands of Europe, such as the Coto de Donana at the mouth of Spain's Rio Guadalquivir, or Romania's Danube Delta or the polders of Wadden Sea in northern Holland.

I can just about conjure its English equivalent from the centuries' long shadows. In the place that I know as Reedham, in late summer was a treetop world drenched in the odour of stale fish and promiscuously splashed with a whitewash of guano. Now the trees where the birds have rebuilt for decades, probably centuries, have eventually died from the rainfall of acid droppings. It makes the stick bundles stand out all the clearer in the staccato canopy and the smooth limbs of the dead snags offer an easy perch for the ungainly long-limbed water birds.

The harsh guttural sounds of parent herons and spoonbills accompany their movements to and from the colony, and their laboured silhouettes constantly traffic above the sky-line. On the other stick platforms young cormorants, awkward and angular pterodactyls snapping at their halo of flies, pick at the sheaths that still enclose their flight feathers. Their bodies are part covered in an innocent sooty down, yet they beat their useless half-feathered wings in readiness, while adult birds lounge at the nest edge, their gular pouches quivering and their wings out-stretched in the hot spring sunshine.

The key thing is that you can't impose this

tremulous heat-hazed scene upon the Reedham of today. The birds are, in a sense, themselves an historical document that not only signifies a lost avifauna, it requires us to re-imagine an entire landscape. The three birds thrive on freshwater fish and other aquatic vertebrates — frogs, newts, water voles or snakes, even — and each demands quite different details. Cormorants dive in the open pools, spoonbills wade through the shallows and sift the muddy shoals, herons stalk along the ditches and wait by the dyke's edge. In combination they imply a rich and varied watery world quite unlike today's valley. We can't recreate the lost place from the presence of the three birds exactly. But we know unequivocally that it was a far wilder and a more natural place, where the river asserted its own rhythms and humans staked their claim to the valley with far less conviction.

★   ★   ★

There is another birdman from the Yare's past, another heir to the traditions established by the builders of that ancient boat in next door's garden. He is far nearer to our time than William Haward or Sir Thomas Browne, and his relationship with the valley's wildlife more closely resembles my own. The

Reverend Richard Lubbock was in that long line of country vicars who were as devoted to their field sports and their fishing rods as they were to the Church or their religious calling. Born in 1798, Lubbock was rector in turn of the parishes of Hellington, Rockland and Bramerton on the south side of the Yare, none of these places much more than an hour's walk from those historic spoonbills at Claxton. The shouelards were long gone by Lubbock's day, but he witnessed a valley still in its prime, and was alive to the forces that were reshaping it even then. In the introduction to his book, *Observations on the Fauna of Norfolk*, Lubbock wrote:

Since I first began to sport about 1816 a marvellous alteration has taken place in Norfolk, particularly in the marshy parts. When first I remember our fens they were full of Terns, Ruffs, and Redlegs [redshank], and yet the old fenmen declared there was not one tenth part of what they remembered when boys. Now, these very parts which were the best, have yielded to the steam engine, and are totally drained — the marshes below Buckenham, which being taken care of were a strong-hold for species when other resorts failed, are now as dry as a bowling green, and oats are grown where seven or eight years back one hundred and twenty-three Snipes were killed in one day by the same gun. The Claxton marshes, which formerly were almost too wet, are now as dry as Arabia.

Just as valuable as Lubbock's own recollections of the Yare's wildlife was his account of the native marshmen who lived at the river's margin. The fenmen were a distinctive breed of Broadland hunter-gatherer, weathering with rustic stoicism the winter's searing easterlies, and then in summer a tertian form of malaria, which they knew as the 'ague'. They made their entire living from the natural products arising out of the wetland and Lubbock felt admiration both of their elemental toughness and of their remarkable fieldcraft. One character he knew 'relied almost entirely on shooting and fishing for the support of himself and family, and lived in a truly primitive manner'. Lubbock's description of this old bushman is full of gentle humour.

'Our broad', as he always called the extensive pool by which his cottage stood, was his microcosm — his world; the islands in it were his gardens of the

Esperides — its opposing extremity his *ultima Thule*. Wherever his thoughts wandered, they could not get beyond the circle of his beloved lake; indeed, I never knew them aberrant but once, when he informed me, with a doubting air that he had sent his wife and his two eldest children to a fair at a country village two miles off, that their ideas might expand by travel; as he sagely observed, they had never been away from 'Our broad'. I went into his house at the dinner hour and found the whole party going to fall most thankfully upon a roasted Herring Gull, killed of course on 'Our broad'.

Lubbock had seen the fenman's annual round of chores at first hand. The short, tough winter days were spent cutting reed, while the cold winter nights offered the chance for a spot of wildfowling by punt (a form of boat not too different from the one in next door's ground). In February he was busy on a network of trimmers, the lines that he wrapped around bundles of floating reed to catch the year's first pike that he could sell at his own back door. By March the eels were in season. So too were lapwings. The eggs of the 'hornpies', as they were known, were highly prized on Georgian and Victorian breakfast tables, not just for their flavour but also for the aesthetics of their exquisite colour and acute pyriform shape.

April was the time for another bird of the open marsh, the ruff. The small pugnacious water birds were renowned for the male's elaborate courtship dress and display, and for being the most expensive bird, ounce for ounce, on the dining table. May twelfth was 'godwit day', celebrating the lanky brick-red waders that almost matched the ruff for high price. As the season wore on, spawning tench were the next crop. It was followed by the marsh hay, rich in wild flowers and known as 'gladdon'. In the late nineteenth century it was a source of food for the horses that used to draw the hansom cabs of the metropolis. One of the stranger ecological links between Victorian London and the Yare were the seeds from the marsh plants picked out of the horse droppings by cockney sparrows in the capital's streets.

Summer was a time for 'flappers' — either young duck without full feathers, or adult birds that were similarly flightless as a result of moult. By late August there was a touch of cold to the evening air, and teal were returning with the curlew and snipe from their northern breeding grounds. By autumn the fenman was as busy acting as a sporting guide to the wealthy — the gentleman gunners, as they were known — as he was hunting for his own larder.

The same cycle of activities had probably constituted the life of fenmen since the time that William Haward and his colleagues investigated the theft of spoonbills in 1300, and almost certainly since long before that. No doubt the villains trespassing on Bardolf's feudal estates at Cantley and Strumpshaw were of much the same stamp as Lubbock's acquaintance living by 'Our broad'. Their mischief probably amounted to nothing more than a little stolen profit to add to the frugal self-sufficiency of their domestic economy.

By Lubbock's day, population growth in the countryside and the reclamation of wetland areas were already placing a squeeze on the age-old lifestyle. There were compensations in the widening public fascination with natural history, since it offered marshmen a new market for collectable specimens of highly sought-after birds, shells or plants. But the increasing commodification of the Yare valley's natural products, their incorporation into capitalist patterns of exploitation, set in train its own negative syndrome. The price for the eggs and skins of rare species simply rose with the animals' ever-increasing scarcity, providing an incentive for the marshmen to carry on until the very last one was gone.

A classic example was the black tern, the small elegant marsh bird of aerial grace and blue-grey plumage. Lubbock recalled it nesting 'in myriads' at a site just north of the Yare in 1818. Within forty years it was extinct in Norfolk and Britain as a whole. The last pair was shot and their final clutch taken; the man who bought both the adults and the eggs was the great Norfolk naturalist Henry Stevenson. One wonders if Stevenson recognised the irony when he subsequently chronicled the black terns' demise in his classic three-volume *Birds of Norfolk?*

Lubbock himself played an unwitting part in the disappearance of the Yare's most celebrated bird, the bittern, that strange owl-brown foghorn of the reedbed. With an insouciance that would in time become legendary he remarked how in 1819 he had shot eleven bitterns in a morning 'without searching particularly for them'.

Even those considered the very commonest birds were also to be affected. The game-dealers in Yarmouth opened up the possibility for marshmen to sell their wild-collected eggs to clients as far away as London. One of the dealers was clearing six or seven hundred eggs a week in the spring and early summer, while in 1821 a single egger from the central Broads area delivered 1,920 lapwing eggs from the marsh. That one man in that one spring period, with his buckets of chocolate-patterned coffee-coloured eggs, was carrying away more lapwings than nested in the entire Norfolk Broads at the end of the twentieth century.

The fragmentary statistics of their wild-caught harvests suggest the relentless pressures latterly imposed by the fenmen. At the same time, those figures are an invaluable measure of the Yare landscape and its wildlife in the nineteenth century. Their importance to me is exactly the same as Sir Thomas Browne's reference to spoonbills, herons and cormorants all nesting in the treetops at Reedham. They open deep vistas into a vanished past.

One of the critical issues they raise is the issue of baselines. When we try to measure the depth, the quality, the richness of our past landscapes, and when we want to see how much we've lost, how far do we pay out the plumb-line to find the bottom? Where exactly should we start to measure our impact upon the land? When we want to re-imagine the old place, in what age should we locate our memories? And what vision of the past do we hold to guide our lives in the present and the future?

The data on our national bird populations are the most thorough statistics for any of our wild communities and are most frequently used to measure qualitative change in the landscape. The information was gathered by that wonderful institution of field science, the British Trust for Ornithology, in two huge surveys, in 1968–72 and again in 1988–91. But it means that the earliest index of environmental alteration is less than forty years old. Is that really where we should begin to calculate the fortunes of our wildlife? Is the Yare of Browne or Lubbock no more than a dream?

Even in the short period since the first 1968 census — effectively, in my own lifetime — I'm aware that the birds of my Yare have sunk lower. I know it not simply because of the BTO's work, but because my neighbour Billy Driver told me so. Billy is another in the Yare clan of hunter-gatherers. He has the steady, rather slow, patient, deeply courteous manner of the Norfolk farm worker and his whole active life was spent on just two large properties abutting the south bank of the Yare at Claxton and Langley, where he was born more than seventy years ago.

In the 1960s Billy developed an interest in birds and started to write down the things he saw. Unlike most of us he didn't just jot down randomly a few names every now and then as the fancy took him. He systematically logged what he saw as he went about his farm work, in the two neighbouring villages, during the course of every single day, for more than twenty years. What started as a routine, perhaps diverting part of his daily life, steadily evolved, with the passage of time, into a meticulous historical record of our parish. In their way, Billy's diaries are as valuable as the journals of Gilbert White. These lists of birds are documents on the place every bit as important as any legal deeds or register of owners, and as you read them you can watch the landscape change.

They serve as a highly magnified and intensely personal prism through which one can observe nationwide changes in bird numbers between the 1960s and 1980s. For some species, Billy's counts become imperceptibly smaller; day by day the names grow steadily more infrequent, until they vanish from his diary altogether. In the twenty years of the journals, species he would once have counted among the most common and typical of the farmlands he worked — grey partridge, snipe, cuckoo, turtle dove, skylark, yellow wagtail, meadow pipit, reed bunting and tree sparrow — disappeared almost completely. Each of these species is, in its turn, an archival document on our past exactly like the spoonbills and the cormorants of Sir Thomas Browne.

★ ★ ★

I line them up now, my community of fellow hunter-gatherers, in chronological order. The ones who built the boat now buried in the ground; the fenmen who robbed the spoonbill nests at Cantley and Strumpshaw and who put William Haward and his colleagues to such trouble; Sir Thomas Browne and Richard Lubbock, with their fenmen and their informants, bring a touch of scholarship to the group; and lastly comes my neighbour Billy Driver and his twenty years of detailed records. With them all here I can see the Yare valley, ultimately, as it should be seen — through time. And through their eyes I can imagine and reimagine what it was and what it's become. Love it as I do, as they must have loved it, I can see also that I live amid a wilderness transformed. And some might say that we have lost more than we have gained.

12

I made my first significant discovery about rooks in the spring of 2003, eighteen months after I'd embarked on the study, and almost two years after we'd moved to the Yare valley. It was modest as discoveries go, but it was mine and it felt like an achievement.

It arose from looking at the birds breeding in and around the valley. Given the sheer size of the night flock gathering at Buckenham Carrs, it seemed logical that the Yare flood plain supported its own substantial resident population, and I wanted to know exactly how many. So I began to count the rookeries in my immediate area and in that spring campaign of 2002 I located nineteen sites. By the following season I'd doubled the number and now I monitor, on an annual basis, a fluctuating but large proportion of forty-five separate rookeries.

What seems equally significant is that I now find it hard *not* to count rookeries. If we go away for a short family visit somewhere — anywhere — it's a reflex response to launch on a largely purposeless sample census. Long car journeys offer another avenue of approach. On several occasions, even when driving, I've found myself, if not counting nests, then counting rookeries. I have full details for the whole of the A1 between Newark and Durham, all transcribed by my elder daughter Rachael. In the handwritten notes she added a few sharp anthropological observations of her own: 'Counting rooks is boring!'

Once my rook obsession was well publicised I found that I didn't have to co-opt family members to the task. Friends volunteered fresh sets of data of their own accord. Tim Dee, on his drive from Bristol to Norwich in late April, gave a complete breakdown of rookeries *en route*, with the number of sites per 80 kilometres travelled. One other totally unexpected revelation has been the number of people who have acquired the rookery-counting habit entirely independently. A near neighbour, now in his eighties, has kept a meticulous record of the four rookeries on his land for almost a quarter of a century.

Even more delightful was the occasion I went to the Suffolk town of Beccles, where there is a minuscule colony of just four pairs near the old market square. I stopped the first likely person coming towards me — white spade beard and sort of rook-appreciating country air — and asked if he knew how long the birds had nested in the middle of town. As long as he could remember. When I enquired if he'd ever counted them — and I had very little hope he'd have a figure — he said, 'No, 'fraid not, but I can tell you how many rookeries there are between here and Diss. Seventeen. All less than a quarter of a mile from the road. I count them every year on my way to work.'

★ ★ ★

When I embarked on my first count of local birds I had as baseline information the report of a Norfolk-wide census of breeding rooks published in 1995. It indicated each parish that held a colony, so it was a case of touring the area until I bumped into the great stick bundles that were starting to appear in the leafless winter landscape.

It was pleasant work. Rookeries aren't difficult to find. They create what are easily the most conspicuous land-bird colonies in Britain, if not all of Europe. This is owing partly to their location and partly to the time of year when rooks start to build. They are among the earliest species to breed, having already paired and even started nest construction by January. Although the main work doesn't usually get under way until February, and at that season they stand out as stick globes in a sky-filled canopy. The task is made easier because rooks don't like the middle of woods. They're birds of shelter belts and tall hedges, roadside avenues, small-scale plantations or, at most, the outer perimeter of a wood. In the Yare valley during the early spring you can spot some from a distance of eight kilometres.

There is an element of challenge about rooking in spring. Even at the most perfunctory level there is an interesting technical test. Somewhere in each clump of trees is a point, a fulcrum, on which the exercise turns, where one can see and work out how to count the nests all around. It sounds straightforward. It's not. The structures seem to move around the moment you look down to check the route or secure your footing. It's one of the reasons I use my mechanical counter. Look upwards again after a few paces and the pattern has become jumbled and you've lost track of those you've counted and those you haven't. You only realise that there's a knack to the business as you complete the counts faster with each new site you visit.

Another initial problem was deciding what was an occupied nest. The issue arose because I originally subscribed to the age-old myth about breeding rooks that they add to the old nests year after year. It's easy to see where the idea comes from. People see the cluster of structures reappearing in the same place each spring and assume that it is not just the same birds, but the same nests, reassembled after a little spring cleaning.

In fact rook nests are not very durable, despite their relatively large size and seemingly solid construction. Unlike the magpie and carrion crow, the rook doesn't insert such a thick mud lining on top of the sticks. In the case of the other two corvids, the mud acts as a form of cement binding the whole structure together and their nests can persist for years. But with rooks the nest is abandoned by early June and throughout the summer it deteriorates. I've found that the autumn and winter storms usually account for all but about a quarter of the nests and those in particularly open-canopied trees are invariably blown down.

Slowly I came to realise that all the nests visible by mid-March to mid-April are new ones assembled by birds intending to breed. Any that survive from the year before are partly or wholly dismantled to supply the sticks for the new build, or the birds build on top of the old one. But an old nest is never taken over as it stands, nor will an old unoccupied structure, except the most vestigial scatter of twigs, survive alongside the new crop of nests.

There are a few exceptions. Evergreen trees offer the most shelter to old nests and slowly over the years they start to accumulate. Continuous stick tenements can form, some running along branches for metres. Working out how many functioning premises there are in these great tangles is devilishly complicated.

I have two other problem rookeries. They are among my favourites and stand in the parish of Thorpe on the southern edge of Haddiscoe Island. I think the key factor that makes them difficult to count is the closeness of the sites to the optimum feeding area, represented by the great grassland expanse just to the north. As a result both colonies are densely populated, leading to the same sort of stick accumulations that one finds in pine trees. There is just too much material left in the trees from previous years for the rooks to cannibalise it all for fresh nests. Gradually, over the years, the trees acquire an accumulating fortress of new and old structures. The place has become so congested that at the periphery rooks now build in hawthorn bushes at half the height of some of their neighbours. But it seems that the squatters would rather occupy these atypical and marginal sites, like shanties on the edge of a bustling city, than forgo the obvious benefits of breeding near Haddiscoe's sea of grass.

★   ★   ★

By the close of the second season of rookery counts I was able to make comparisons between my figures for twenty-one locations and those from 1995. Two key facts stood out. In the intervening nine years (the 1995 census reflected counts from both that year and the season before) breeding rooks had increased from 1,333 pairs to 1,916, a rise of 43.7 per cent.

The other striking discovery was the importance of a narrow band that runs all along the old beach line on the lower Yare and Waveney valleys. These gentle inclines are clothed in belts of fen woodland dominated by coppiced alder. The wood strips aren't continuous but where they are substantial they house rookeries. There are eight colonies on the northern shore of the Yare flood plain and thirteen on the opposite shore along the edge of the Yare-Waveney complex. Together they hold 2,650 pairs, more than a sixth of all the breeding rooks logged for Norfolk in 1995.

Equally significant was the size of the colonies. The average for all twenty-one rookeries was 126 pairs, two and a half times the average for the county and more than five times the national average (24.4), when the entire British rook population was last surveyed in 1975. The latter census marked the nadir in rook fortunes during the twentieth century and the average rookery size has probably never been smaller. A further partial British census in the mid-nineties established that rook numbers had risen in the intervening twenty years by 39 per cent. Even so, the Yare valley figures suggested that substantially higher densities existed here than almost anywhere else in Britain. The only counties where the average rookery size was higher during the 1975 census were in north-east Scotland. The Aberdeenshire figure, for example, was 139.1, the highest in all Britain, reflecting the fact that the region holds the world's highest known densities of rooks.

Examining the figures more closely I saw that there was another more intriguing story inside the full Yare-valley spread of data. There are two discontinuous strips of largely alder-oak carr on either side of the river. Both border the great sea of grass of Halvergate Marshes and Haddiscoe Island. The strip on the west side of this grassland block runs for about 1.5 kilometres north from the church in the village of Reedham. The other 2.5-kilometre belt lies on the south side of the Yare between the villages of Haddiscoe and Lower Thurlton. In combination the two areas of riverine woodland hold seven rookeries. Their average size is 235 pairs and collectively they house 1,646 pairs, accounting for more than 60 per cent of the entire Yare-valley total.

It made sense. This bird of the steppe loves grassland. The Yare valley holds the biggest surviving patch of lowland grassland in England. The valley is therefore a great place for rooks, with the highest densities in East Anglia. As I said at the outset, it was hardly a major discovery. But no one else had noticed it and I was well satisfied.

★ ★ ★

There is another major satisfaction in counting rook nests that I hadn't bargained for when I embarked on the exercise. The inhabitants of the rookery are most active at that point in the year when winter veers away and when the British landscape finally tilts downhill towards us in all its temperate softness.

It is that moment when the earth and our own bones — and our loins — loosen. Small wonder that the rooks' sky-scraping colony with all its hectic and turbulent clamour comes to our minds as a constant metaphor for life's reawakening. Edward Thomas captured it beautifully in his quatrain 'Thaw'.

Over the land freckled with snow half-
thawed
The speculating rooks at their nests cawed
And saw from elm-tops, delicate as flower
of grass.
What we below could not see, Winter
pass.

Rooks catch a glimpse of sex and summer even when the frost lies on the bare woodland floor.

My annual tour of all the Yare-valley rookeries has acquired an almost formal character, like calling on old friends, each in turn, during a home visit. I think of it now as a yearly rite, a beating of the bounds for the whole of my territory, and it gives me a sensation of having cheated nature, of acquiring an extra season within a season.

It's that early or pre-spring few weeks when

everything around is entering the phase of rebirth, but before the full-blown mood of life floods across the landscape in a tide of greenery and birdsong. Rookery time comes just before the summer migrants return, although I cherish the first swallow, or the flimsy flip-flap notes of male chiffchaffs or, more startling, a breezy salad-fresh spurt of blackcap song, as important way-markers in the process.

It is a season made up of very particular moments. It brings the year's first conscious sightings of *Xanthoria calcicola*, that church-going lichen of graveyards and headstones which somehow never looks so gloriously yolk-yellow until the sun shines. It's a time of sun-warmed pools of ground ivy, of black-thorn blossom, or stitchwort and the primroses' flaring yellow in hedge banks so severely pruned they look like the shaven heads of US marines.

It brings the first giant queen buff-tailed bumblebees who, still drugged from their winter hibernation and testing the newfound power of their wings, career though the dew-edged grasses like wild boar charging in the woods. It coincides also with the first tender cycle of young rabbits, some so tiny they seem barely able to part the wet grass as they flee. Even the smoky hanks of fur left by the burrow entrance seem filled with a sense of promise.

With each fresh visit to a site there come those microscopically small encounters with fragments of the landscape that possibly only I might have noticed or can recall from year to year. In total, the details create the sense of a private relationship with a countryside that has become, over the centuries, more shared and public than any in the world. At Halvergate, for instance, by Hospital Carr, I bow to the line of pollarded willows. I know that at that point in the lopped torso where the hedgehog's back of fresh growth erupts, there is also a beetle-gnawed hollow where the dead leaves gather through winter.

At Wickhampton, behind the Church Farm barns, there is an odd sort of pleasure in greeting once more the smashed horse-chestnut stumps and the dead octopus-limbed sycamore where, despite all this infirmity, the rooks still build and breed. Nearby I like to rootle around in one old lean-to barn for the winter's crop of barn owl pellets, those compacted black lozenges that are the cast remains from the bird's digestive tract; hieroglyphs on life's mystery straight from the gut of an owl. Although it's open on one side, the building's old flint-faced walls and worm-riddled timbers have perhaps held on to that immensely comforting reek of cattle and straw for 150 years. I like the idea of a truly ancient aroma. I love the idea that in all the world no one else has seen and smelt and relished the details of this unwatched, unconscious place.

By the path to Decoy Carr at Reedham there is the fortress nest of a carrion crow in an alder's crown. It's been unused now for twenty-four months but it still resists decay. As I pass I recall that in the year of its construction the twig ends sprouting from its wicker walls were at the same state of bud as those on the living tree, and *en masse* they gave to the bare canopy — and to the crow's nest itself — the faintest bloom of glaucous green.

In Decoy Carr itself I can discover all over again the python coils of ivy around the oak bolls where the bluebells grow, the sycamore heartwood returned to dust by beetle, the huge plates of peat lifted skywards with the gale-felled birch. In all these moments of woodland intimacy, the bare trees rising sheer on all sides, I cannot avoid the feeling of a landscape watching. It fills me with a curious but delicious sensation that somehow I am not alone. I move through the trees, almost self-consciously, and all around the shadows of the rooks swirl in a perpetual cycle that is tied to my own brief passage below.

13

It may be *Corvus frugilegus* that draws me from my bed at dawn throughout the winter. It's certainly the black bird of flesh and blood keeping me out on the marsh until the sun sinks to its rose-tainted grave on an autumn evening, but it's an entirely different creature that had me scouring through the literature. The bird I hunted across several centuries and numerous volumes of past encyclopaedia and old county avifauna, in copies of ancient journals and verse anthologies of a particular vintage, was a very distinct entity. The two types of bird occasionally mingled, but gradually I began to see this imagined rook of folklore and myth, the rook encountered in poetry and nature writing, as an animal with an independent life and ecology that was every bit as interesting as its real-life shadow.

For my first meeting with what I might call the 'inner rook', I have my father to thank. It was more than thirty-five years ago and I was around ten years old. But I can remember his story vividly. It was one of those tales where the exact relationship of the witness to the narrated events was lost or blurred with the retelling. As I recall, my father said it was a friend who'd seen them, but it might just as easily have been a friend of a friend ... and so on.

The person had been driving from our home town, Buxton in Derbyshire, over what we call locally the Longhill, a route which follows the A5004 towards Manchester. Skirting the eastern edge of the Goyt valley, it is a picturesque drive slowed considerably by a sequence of sharp bends and long, awkward curves. But at intervals you're offered relief from the twisting route by occasional wide panoramas of the walled pasture, either falling away or climbing steeply on one side or the other.

My father's friend claimed that as he made his way along the road he suddenly came upon a gathering of rooks configured in a clear wide circle in one of those open stretches of field. At the centre of the ring were two or three other rooks apparently surrounded and being subjected to scrutiny by their fellow birds. He was deeply puzzled by the behaviour, by the distinct choreography in their positions and the sense of formal transaction between the various parties. An image of the birds clearly remained with him while he continued with his affairs, because on his return to Buxton via Longhill, he made a specific point of scrutinising the spot where he'd first seen them.

There to his astonishment were several black-feathered corpses, at exactly the point in the open fields where the original rooks had been surrounded by their fellow birds. It was so macabre that he got out and walked over. There was no mistaking it. The victims were covered in death blows, mortal wounds rained down upon them with that bone-hilted pickaxe bill, and all the more shocking for having been inflicted by their own kind. While my father rounded off his tale of the mysterious inner life of a bird, I imagined the horror of it — the lifeless bundles lying on the damp evening grass, the shadows lengthening along the dark gritstone walls, and the flies buzzing in their long, mazy spirals down upon the dead.

★ ★ ★

Among the many tens or hundreds of thousands of stories I've heard or read since the occasion of my father's tale, that five-minute account of the rook 'parliament' held sufficient power for it to have been logged away for over thirty-five years. Now I think I can see why the story should have survived intact for so long.

167

I was ten or eleven. My interest in wildlife was just then assuming in embryonic form the shape it's had for the last three decades. Birds and animals were gradually emerging from their childhood guise as friendly characters in stories and books, with names like Chicken Licken and Brer Rabbit and personalities and clothes and the other various attributes of human children. Instead they were acquiring the genuine characteristics and the physical features which seemed so beautifully delineated in my first library of field guides. I was both detaching myself from them as friends, and re-engaging with them as expressions of some new-found and compelling otherness in nature.

Suddenly, with my father's tale of an avian court and rook punishment, the distinction between the two was blurred. Here was totally fresh and shocking information — and what child could challenge the natural-historical authority of two adults — that birds spoke in their own kind of language and consulted one another and reflected on each other's actions. They held moral views of their fellows' conduct, had leaders with powers to assemble the flock, strict codes of behaviour, perhaps passed down for generations, which sometimes required that transgressions be judged and punished. If necessary, if the crimes were so heinous, then

168

the birds — which were already embedded in my imagination as symbols of a wilder and freer life — would behave just as adult humans did. In fact they were worse. They did something that, I was aware even at ten, we did not. They took another's life in retribution.

For years the tale was stored in a limbo section of my own mental landscape, not serving as concrete data to be worked securely into my understanding of the world; but neither was it dismissed out of hand. It remained there, uncatalogued and mysterious, waiting for fresh discoveries to confirm or refute it, until it finally found its way into that great attic storeroom of unclassifiable myth marked childhood.

★   ★   ★

My own early encounter with the rook of our imagination makes me appreciate just how enticing the creature can be. Throughout our 5,000-year-old relationship with the species its mythic twin has given rise to a whole cycle of stories and fables, but what is striking is that the tales are told in a peculiarly English accent. When the writer Aubrey Seymour suggested that the rook's hoarse call has 'an essence of Old England about it', he may have been paying unconscious homage to this ancient national trait.

It's not difficult to see how the bird made such an appeal to our powers of invention. Just consider that astonishing call. So coarse and inarticulate in the single bird, it is magically transformed into something strangely euphonious and endlessly suggestive when heard in aggregate, or at a distance. Gilbert White was deeply alive to the charm: '[it] becomes a . . . pleasing murmur,' he wrote, 'very engaging to the imagination, and not unlike the cry of a pack of hounds in hollow, echoing woods, or the rushing of the wind in tall trees, or the tumbling of the tide upon a pebbly shore.'

Our overriding perception of those raucous, clattering notes is that they constitute a form of conversation. Writers frequently make comparisons between rook vocalisations and our own voices. The poet W.S. Graham, hearing the birds in his adopted Cornish village of Madron, wrote in 'The Word's Name' that 'The talking rooks across/ The white Winter put/ Their noisy flying language.'

Sometimes it almost seems as if the silence that lies between our respective languages might be bridged in some way. Just before the Battle of Loos in northern France during the First World War, the aspiring poet Charles

Sorley — he wrote just thirty-seven completed poems in a tragically brief life — had a small notebook of verse in his army knapsack. One poem read:

There, where the rusty iron lies,
The rooks are cawing all the day.
Perhaps no man, until he dies,
Will understand them, what they say.

The evening makes the sky look clay.
The slow wind waits for night to rise.
The world is half content. But they

Still trouble all the trees with cries,
That know, and cannot put away,
The yearning to the soul that flies
From day to night, from night to day.

Perhaps we shouldn't be surprised that death had been preying on the mind of a young soldier. Even so, it seems eerie that the very next day the twenty-year-old was killed by a sniper's bullet. Sorley's personal reflection on rook sounds articulates the wider impression, even the hope, that at some level the birds are talking to us, and if only we could understand them, secrets about life and ourselves would be unlocked.

The idea that this black bird has some

strange prophetic power over human life has lost none of its appeal today. Dave Gregory and Andy Partridge, songwriters for the New Wave band, XTC, produced an album, *Nonsuch*, in 1991. The track entitled 'Rook' has the following lyric:

Rook, rook
Read from your book
Who murders who and where is the treasure hid?

. . .

Rook, rook
Gaze in the brook
If there's a secret can I be part of it?
Crow, crow
Before I'll let go, say is that my name on the bell?
Soar up high, see the semaphore from the washing lines
Break the code of the whispering chimneys and traffic signs
What's the message that's written under the base of clouds?

The other rook characteristic underpinning our anthropomorphic projections is the bird's profoundly sociable life. It seems so much a mirror of our own. In an older England the species closely replicated the geographical spread of the human population across the countryside, with almost a rookery and village to every parish. Poets and natural history writers repeatedly drew parallels between the two communities. The rookery was variously described as an 'airy city' (James Thomson), 'an asylum' (William Shenstone), and 'a sweet sylvan village' (Isaac Williams), while Richard Jefferies developed the comparison further: 'In early days men seem to have frequently dug their entrenchments or planted their stockades on the summit of hills. To the rooks their trees are their hills, giving security from their enemies. The wooden houses in the two main streets are evidently of greater antiquity than those erected in the outlying settlements . . . But the nests forming the principal streets are piled up to a considerable height — fresh twigs being added every year.'

It was not just that rooks mimicked the physical structure of human society, it was that they appeared to share a comparable social order. In his poem 'Aylmer's Field', Tennyson touched on the idea of an innate democratic spirit governing rook lives when he wrote 'as dawn/ Aroused the black republic on his elms'. The concept of equality didn't exclude some type of corvid-style leadership. In 'Locksley Hall', Tennyson famously referred to this dominant individual as 'the many-winter'd crow who leads the clanging rookery home'.

It was presumably one of the responsibilities of the aged bird to appoint another widely credited rook figure, the 'sentinel' or 'guard'. This critical flock member was said to stand at the edge of feeding groups to keep a sharp watch for danger. The existence of this avian watchman was almost proverbial at all levels of rural society for centuries. Thomas Bewick, the man who gave his name to the swan and was a pioneer wildlife artist of the late eighteenth century, knew all about the sentinel. In his *History of British Birds* (1797), Bewick's woodcut plate includes a detailed close-up of an individual adult, but the background landscape contains almost as much information about rooks as the main portrait. On the left hand of his central figure, Bewick depicted in miniature a large feeding flock spread across a ploughed field. Standing high above and distinctly visible on the topmost twigs of the nearest tree is just one watchful bird, the sentinel.

The man who finally unravelled the matter, Edmund Selous, was a scrupulously observant naturalist in his own right. He spent many days observing rook responses to disturbance and eventually concluded that the way in which the alarm spread through a flock was entirely random and that no single bird gave warning as a kind of duty.

It may seem odd, but I find it strangely comforting to discover that Selous' conclusions haven't yet filtered through to all of us. During the course of my work on this book I received a letter that read: 'My brother-in-law, who has spent a long life living and working on farms and in the woods of Kent, maintains that each rookery has a sentinel perched on the top of the tallest tree in the rookery, on guard. He also believes that, should the sentinel be shot, the whole rookery would be abandoned.'

★   ★   ★

It is interesting to observe that the great age of the 'inner rook' was from the mid-nineteenth until the early twentieth century, coinciding with the wider flowering of natural history itself among the Victorian public. A long sequence of eminent naturalists published multi-volume works about Britain's wildlife and birds in particular; William Macgillivray(1837), Charles Waterton (1838), William Yarrell (1842), Sir William Jardine, Robert Gray (1871), Henry Seebohm (1883) and the Reverend F.O. Morris (1895) are only a sample. In their accounts of the rook each subscribed to one fragment or another of the overall fictional persona. In turn the occasional credulity of these more scholarly ornithologists seems to have licensed the unrestrained fabrication of other nineteenth-century writers, whose stock in trade was a natural world peopled with animal characters exactly like those I'd encountered in the *Adventures of Brer Rabbit*.

It was these Victorian sentimentalists who routinely peddled the bird cloaked in juridical black, who arranged him into 'parliaments', and watched him dispense justice or punishment, dismantle the nests of trespassers and post sentinels or appoint leaders to preside over the flock.

The Reverend Bosworth Smith is a classic example. In his *Bird Life and Bird Lore*, this 'Late Fellow of Trinity College, Oxford, and formerly assistant master of Harrow School' recorded the observations of his equally fanciful friend, Dr J.Brunton Blaikie:

[He] has described to me the proceedings of a remarkable convocation of rooks which he was able to watch from close at hand. One day, in the month of August, he noticed a number of rooks approaching the trees of a small rookery

176

in front of his house, which, at that time of year, were seldom visited by them. One of the rooks, flying about ten yards in front of the others, carried in its bill a twig, some eighteen inches long. It took up a prominent position on one of the trees, deposited the twig on the branch by its side, and then the business of the meeting began. First, one rook would talk in what seemed to be a set speech, and then they would all suddenly strike in, with a clamorous assent or dissent. Then, a second rook would address the meeting, whether to second the motion, or to propose an amendment to it, and his peroration would be received or objected to in like manner. But the most interesting thing about it all was that the twig-bearer seemed to be the president of the assembly. The twig must have been a badge of office, like the spear of the auctioneer at Rome, or his hammer in England. It was like the Speaker's mace or the judge's black cap, a symbol, a something held in reserve. After half an hour, when the business was finished, and, as it would seem, the 'noes had it', the president picked up the twig, dissolved the assembly, and, followed by the rank and file, departed, in the opposite direction to that in which they had come . . . a quarter of a mile away.

It is hard now to imagine what genuine avian behaviour — if these writers saw anything at all — could possibly have accounted for the detailed descriptions in such instances. One wonders if behind some of the more extravagant inventions we should see the sad simian face of Charles Darwin, and the cold, hard machinery of his natural selection clanking inexorably in the background. Perhaps the most human of birds held out the faintest possibility of some more sympathetic, even mutual relationship with nature. The rook with his jurisprudence and his moral sense and his innately democratic instincts offered the hope that we might not be entirely alone. As the planet performed its utterly indifferent evolutions through time and space, how pleasant to think that some small portion of the natural world might just have a human soul.

★   ★   ★

Undoubtedly the rook virtue that the English took most to their hearts was the birds' apparent loyalty to home. A colony's dependable recreation of the rookery, year in year out, seemed to express as deep a homing instinct for our green and pleasant land as the English felt themselves. And it was not so much that they were territorial about their patch; it was more that the rooks were seen as belonging to the land, for better and for worse. The Scottish naturalist Sir William Jardine pointed out that 'Villages and towns have, in many instances, arisen around their colonies, but the inhabitants will only quit their venerable resting place on the removal of the trees themselves, and if left thus unmolested, will continue to assemble at their stated times and perform their allotted duties, seemingly unconscious of the most crowded and noisy thoroughfares.'

Occasionally the attachment was tested to the limit. Reverend Frank Morris, the most credulous of all the nineteenth-century rook-watchers, claimed that he knew a Yorkshire estate where the birds were banished by gamekeepers who maintained a constant barrage of gunfire at the nest site. The rooks found a way of keeping faith with the land, nevertheless, running up forty nests one Sunday while the keepers were in church.

Morris' tale of eviction was hardly the norm. In fact, the reverse was the case. The sector of English society that felt the deepest appreciation of the rooks' blood ties to the land was itself the landed gentry. During the nineteenth century the rook was more than anything a bird of the country estate. Look carefully at Bewick's rook woodcut and there, just behind his bird's mantle, is the outline of a manor house nestled among its laager of protective trees, with the rookery nests threaded like gems through the canopy. All of the period's author-naturalists remarked on the relationship. Several of them — Sir William Jardine, Charles Waterton and Lord Lilford — had rookeries on their own properties. The latter claimed that there were as many as 1,500-2,000 pairs within a five-kilometre radius of Lilford, his Northamptonshire seat, and possibly as many as 4,000, which would have made it as much a rook heaven as the Yare valley.

The attachment was all the more striking because it flew in the face of apparent self-interest. Rooks had a long-standing status as agricultural pests, whose persecution was required by English law. There were compensatory protein and sport to be had from the annual rook shoot, but such economic benefit doesn't begin to explain the deep-rooted fondness for the bird. Many country houses looked on the rookery with far more than pride. Often it was a type of status symbol, and in the 1890s, for those landowners who were not so blessed, the magazine *The Field,* which was standard reading in the drawing rooms of most Victorian country piles, carried articles and correspondence on 'How to Form a Rookery'. Sometimes the laird's love-affair with his birds became a source of social tension in the rural community. Hugh Gladstone records a case of over a hundred farmers petitioning the local gentry to put their rooks down.

The Bishop Edward Stanley, a naturalist-clergyman even more unwilling than the Reverend Morris to clutter a good tale with the facts, tells a story from revolutionary France that is so bizarre it might just be the truth. But whether it's fact or fiction is almost immaterial to the light it sheds on the fundamental psychological associations between the rooks, the land and its upper-class owners. 'When their dreadful Revolution broke out,' Stanley wrote:

accompanied with murder and bloodshed which can never be forgotten, the country people, amongst other causes of dissatisfaction with their superiors, alleged their being fond of having rookeries near their houses; and, in one instance, a mob of these misguided and ignorant people proceeded to the residence of the principal gentleman in their neighbourhood, from whence they dragged him, and hung his body upon a gibbet, after which they attacked the rookery, and continued to shoot the Rooks amidst loud acclamations.

Even the Reverend Morris appreciated the ecological facts that underpinned the rooks' true fealty to the landed estate. 'Rooks build,' he suggested, 'in the vicinity of old mansions or other buildings, chiefly, as I imagine, on account of ancient and fullgrown trees being the accompaniment of these.' In Dumfriesshire at the turn of the nineteenth century, Hugh Gladstone gave a systematic breakdown of the rookeries in the county, which emphasised the bird's overwhelming dependence upon the laird's love of mature trees. Almost all the big rookeries were in the grounds of country seats and one of them was believed to date back to 1640. The largest in the region, in fact one of the largest in Britain at the time, was a further telling expression of the symbiosis existing between the aristocracy and *Corvus frugilegus*.

It was the rookery on the estate of Sir William Jardine. Jardine was one of the great naturalists of the mid-Victorian age and at twenty-one inherited a large red sandstone property called Jardine Hall to the north-east of Dumfries. In its prime the house and its birds made a simultaneous impression. A friend of Jardine recalled how, 'before he got to the hall door', a visitor would have his attention 'drawn to an enormous quantity of rooks wheeling over a beautiful half circle of trees spreading to the grass beneath, making him think the place were alive with birds and game.'

When I visited one cold January afternoon the house had long been demolished and the remaining blocks of stone that marked its location were raked by showers of frozen rain. There were still many magnificent beech and oak trees lining the approach road from the south, and closer to the surviving outbuildings was a lovely beech hedge thick with copper leaves and moss-coated stems that resembled green-furred serpents writhing down into the earth. The most impressive structure was the old stable made of the same local Annandale stone (from which Jardine extracted fossilised footprints of marine turtles that must have walked through the red ooze millions of years ago). Its clock had stopped at 9.30 exactly, and on the cupola-shaped roof was a weather vane dated 1825; it was my only glimpse of Sir William and his rooks.

The weather vane was erected just four

years after Jardine inherited the family seat, by which date the rookery was already deemed to be ancient. The colony was mentioned in the 1853 edition of White's *Natural History of Selborne* which Jardine had edited, when the birds numbered anything up to 2,000 pairs. Today there aren't any at the original site and the nearby farm has just 83 pairs. The passing of the Jardines seems to have foreshadowed the doom of the birds themselves.

During the heyday of Jardine Hall, however, the reverse notion was more widely believed. Rooks nesting around a country manor were thought to have insight into the destiny of its human occupants. 'Verily,' wrote the knowing Reverend Bosworth Smith, 'the rook sees far more than we give him credit for seeing, hears more than we think that he hears, thinks more than we think that he thinks.' 'Last year,' he added, 'the rooks in the rookery of the Grange, Lord Ashburton's house near Alresford, [Hampshire] . . . left, in a body, their nests and nestlings, and have not since returned. The villagers predicted disaster to the family or neighbourhood, and disaster promptly came.'

This forewarning of doom was virtually a speciality of the species. Proofs of the rooks' gift of second sight were everywhere in

Victorian publications. 'A singular circumstance is reported,' ran one typical account, 'in connection with the recent suicide of Mr Graves, of Linwood Grange. Near the house a colony of rooks had established themselves, and, on the day of the funeral, immediately on the appearance of the hearse, the birds left the locality in a body, deserting their nests, all of which contained young.'

★   ★   ★

In some ways I've come to envy these observers of the inner rook. Their birds seem so much more expressive than mine. Theirs are not anchored in a great body of observed detail. The facts don't weigh them down. The birds that once wove their enchanted circle of nests around the country house trafficked freely between some other realm and their human neighbours, carrying portents or messages about a moral order inherent in nature, or trailing the possibility of metempsychosis. Their birds seem graced with so much more magic than the ones I watch.

Yet the English park is one locality where the real bird and the inner rook still meet. Modern ecologists attempting to explain the consistent pattern of landscape features evident in the country park suggest that this idealised form of environment — with its elevated views usually across water, and its wide sweep of open grassland broken here and there by groves of tall trees — is actually African in origin. Such a landscape is thought to be an attempt to recreate the first Eden where we once climbed down from the trees, raised ourselves off all fours and walked on our hind legs for the first time upon the Earth. It's a version of the open African savannah where the human odyssey began.

By chance, rooks have also found that the various characteristics of parkland also match their own version of the optimum environment. The sociable African primate and the gregarious Asian crow converge ecologically in the grounds of the typical country house. The rook has thus become a symbol of our most deeply held ideals about landscape. For the British, at least, it is the bird of paradise.

14

My discovery of the large breeding population of rooks concentrated around Halvergate
and Haddiscoe had been a major source of
satisfaction. But it wasn't an end in itself.
Rooking in spring was really a secondary
part of my mission and almost a form of
displacement activity in the one season when
rooks don't gather to roost at all. It had
established the base materials from which the
Buckenham Carrs assembly was constituted,
but my real quest was to understand the roost
itself in all its parts. I was entranced by those
evening flights, the birds scattered like
patterns of iron filings across the metallic sky
of winter, but what was the magnet drawing
them heavenwards? The key question I
wanted to answer was *why* they roosted.

It was precisely the mystery of it that had
set my natural history on its new course, as
I described in Chapter 6, but I had little
real insight into how I'd settle the problem.
I'm not a natural scientist. I couldn't
undertake experiments in laboratory conditions to test a hypothesis, nor could I trap
the birds and ring or wing-tag them for

individual identification. I simply hoped that if I visited the banks of the river and watched them gather often enough, somehow the truth might fall from its tree like an overripe apple.

When I examined the literature it was equally apparent that the *why* of roosts was the question others had found the most difficult to answer. However, the *what* of roosts — the way the birds gathered, the time they flew, the means of assembly, the places and seasons that they did it — had been appreciated for hundreds of years.

A vision of corvids in dark trains across the winter sky is so embedded in our national psyche that it's proverbial. The expression, 'as the crow flies', that linear measurement of distance through or, perhaps, over a landscape, is clearly a response to the direct, purposeful and conspicuous flight lines of rooks as they converge on their evening destination. In pre-industrial times, before the wrist-watch was a birthright, the birds' outward and homeward processions acted as the slow-swinging metronome for the agricultural day. Farm workers used rook flights as a means of knowing exactly when to down tools.

Poets too had long observed and written on rook roosts. One of the best early references is in Shakespeare's *Macbeth*, on the eve of his murder of Duncan, when the eponymous thane registers the fall of dusk with the words: 'Light thickens, and the crow makes wing to th' rooky wood.' As usual Shakespeare proved an observant naturalist. He appreciated not only the timing of roost flights — they occur exactly, as he so memorably put it, when 'light thickens' — but also that the location was in Birnam Wood.

Rook roosts are invariably deep inside woods. This may seem an obvious point, but remember rooks aren't woodland birds. They're creatures of the grass. They need trees only for certain purposes. It is precisely their choice of a habitat seldom visited by the species which provides strong evidence of the roost's special function, including protection from the elements and security from predators.

There are occasional exceptions to the woodland rule. There's a major roost on the west side of Norwich, which regularly rivals Buckenham Carrs' for size, where the birds use no more than a small plantation adjacent to a private fishing lake. But the undisturbed conditions created by the site's tightly controlled access enhance its attractiveness as a roost. Buckenham Carrs, it should be noted, is also a privately owned wood from which the public are firmly excluded, a key factor, probably, in both its size and persistence.

The most striking anomaly to the roost-in-woodland rule was a gathering that occurred near Wigtown in south-west Scotland for just a single winter in 1970-71. The temporary flowering of this assembly had much to do with the intense cold of that particular time and it was thought to comprise birds moving into the area from further east, including many continental refugees. It numbered as many as 50,000 birds, possibly the second largest ever recorded in Britain.

In 2005 I went to see the site. Even on the map there was an air of improbability about Outtle Well Plantation, which looked little more than a sliver of green running for a couple of kilometres alongside the B7004 before the road arrived at the coastal hamlet of Garlieston. As I drove by, I realised that the incongruence between setting and spectacle was even greater than I'd imagined. It was less a plantation, more a wide hedge border, and it was difficult to see how so many birds, so much intensity of life, had squeezed each night into that confined corridor. Collectively a flock of 50,000 would weigh about 15 tonnes, and the adjacent road must have been bespattered white from their nightly droppings while the sea-roar of calls would have drowned the sound of passing cars. I tried to envisage the rank of beech trees, now locked in an iron-grey stillness, once clothed in its kaleidoscopic foliage of winter black.

The site had been discovered by an innovative project by Scottish ornithologists in the 1970s to map all the corvid roosts across the country. There were 140 spread evenly in all areas where rooks were distributed, with a concentration and some of the largest examples in Aberdeenshire. English and Welsh bird-watchers have never attempted to replicate this ambitious survey, but it seems inconceivable that roosts aren't as evenly distributed across the countryside south of the border. Many of the largest in each county are certainly well known to local birders. My guess is that most Britons who live in a rural setting — and even many city-dwellers — can step into their back gardens on a January afternoon before sunset and observe some aspect of the corvid roost.

This ubiquity of roosts was in itself part of my Damascene conversion to rooks. I became aware that for forty years a complex unfolding ritual beauty had been on offer and I'd never once stopped to observe it. Once

191

attuned, however, I recognised the wider implications: mystery was threaded into the very fabric of my everyday world, if only I chose to notice.

★ ★ ★

One of those who'd already noticed was the poet John Clare. In his long poem of the 1820s entitled 'The Shepherd's Calendar', the Northamptonshire writer described a corvid gathering he'd observed in the vicinity of Whittlesey just to the south-east of Peterborough.

> Whilst many a mingled swarthy crowd —
> Rook, crow, and jackdaw — noising loud,
> Fly to and fro to dreary fen,
> Dull winter's weary flight again;
> They flop on heavy wings away
> As soon as morning wakens grey,
> And, when the sun sets round and red,
> Return to naked woods to bed.

I suspect every one of the world's forty-odd members of the genus *Corvus* exhibit some roosting instinct, but the British species all certainly associate in roosts just as Clare described. Even ravens join them, but jackdaws are particularly constant partners. I doubt if there has ever been a British 'rook' roost where they were not present. There seems to be a deep ecological attachment between the two species, amounting almost to mutualism, that exceeds almost any other avian partnership in Europe and has been largely unexamined by ecologists.

Another typically accurate detail in Clare's passage is that the corvid roost appears in his description of his shepherd's January round of activities, and at precisely the moment when roosts reach their annual maximum. However, roosts are far from permanent and go into steep decline even by late winter. In mid-March they have vanished completely. By that date rooks have transferred their night-time allegiance from the roost to the rookery. In fact the species' entire life is a constant oscillation between these central fixtures — roost and rookery.

The two sites function in the following basic pattern. The place where the birds nest each year is of central importance from late February or early March to June, the period of the rooks' entire breeding cycle. (I have been amazed to find that this basic temporal pattern holds true for rooks breeding in Spain or Turkey, as it does in Norfolk and Aberdeenshire.) During these spring months

193

the birds spend all their days and nights either in the nest trees themselves or transporting nest material and food to them. Once the young birds fledge and embark on an independent existence, the rookery ceases to exert the same hold on the rook family's daily life.

Instead, for the next eight months — from June to the following February — they show attachment to a second location. This roost site is the one to which they will return every evening and leave at dawn, sometimes travelling up to 32 kilometres to the daytime feeding areas. The pattern continues until spring, when rooks abandon the roost once more, transferring allegiance back to the rookery as soon as the female has started to incubate her eggs.

Into this simple binary pattern I need to introduce some complexity. While rooks show no interest whatsoever in the roost site as soon as they start nesting, once they cease to breed and resume their nightly return to the roost, they don't entirely abandon association with the rookery. From August onwards they may resume visits to the rookery for short periods every day, even gathering on their nest trees towards dusk before flying off to the roost. In short, the psychological attractions of the rookery persist in the non-breeding period.

A second complication is that rooks may use two roosts in sequence (possibly even three, although I have never recorded it) during the non-breeding period. From June they may occupy a first site, and then at some later date, usually in the autumn, they transfer allegiance to another roost, which is used through the winter. The sequence of shifting geographical attachments from rookery to sub-roost then to the main roost involves a parallel process of numerical concentration. A roost draws birds from several or even many surrounding rookeries. Equally a major roost like Buckenham Carrs draws in all the rooks and jackdaws from all the surrounding sub-roosts.

The birds' loyalty to a roost while it is *the* functioning night-time sanctuary can be as complete as it seems to me totally arbitrary. The point is well illustrated by a situation in the Yare valley. You would imagine that the rooks from the rookeries that are closest to Buckenham Carrs would inevitably use that site as their roost as soon as they finished breeding. But they don't. Instead from mid-June until mid-September they fly to a sub-roost called Mulberry Carr on the south side of the Yare — i.e. on the opposite side of the valley (see the map on p. x). This logic is strangest in birds from a small rookery just 400 metres from Buckenham. These rooks, along with others from colonies to the north, fly away from or even directly over Buckenham to get to Mulberry Carr. I've never seen a single bird deviate from the pattern and stay north of the river. Conversely, once Mulberry Carr is abandoned it remains unused until the following June.

The first naturalist to give careful thought to the dynamic relationship between rookery and roost was a young English Quaker scholar called Wilfred Backhouse Alexander, working in Oxfordshire. He wrote up the results of a pioneering study in a paper entitled 'The Rook Population of the Upper Thames Region', published in a fledgling volume of the *Journal of Animal Ecology* (1930). The author had just been appointed director of the Oxford Bird Census, a prototype of the sort of population studies which are now the common currency of the British Trust for Ornithology. In the 1920s the post made Alexander Britain's original professional field ornithologist.

He was the first to state emphatically that the wider pool of birds represented in a rook roost was itself a discrete community with shared feeding areas and other common patterns of behaviour. In the decade prior to his Oxford appointment Alexander had worked among the wider and wilder horizons of the Australian outback and he settled on 'tribe' as a word to describe the larger rook community of which the roost was composed. In his paper he wrote of the 'tribal affinities' of members of the same roost. The idea was subsequently refined and another expression — one perhaps more congenial to the English rural setting — was chosen in its place. It was thus a *parish* of rooks which entered the corvophiles' lexicon and invoked the overall territory from which the birds drained each evening into the nocturnal sanctuary.

Alexander also gave consideration to one of the issues that I find most compelling and mysterious: the process by which a roost site is selected. He suggested that it was invariably in or near an existing rookery. There seems to have been some general folk awareness of the fact long before Alexander's work, because in Lancashire, at least, a site that was both rookery and roost was known locally as a 'Royal Rookery'. The description is apt because large rookeries are often exactly the sites selected. The classic example is at Hatton Castle in Aberdeenshire. This wooded park near the town of Turriff boasts the largest ever single roost recorded in Britain, a 1971 total of 65,000 birds. The roost exists today, although it is much reduced in size. It also happens to have been the largest rookery ever recorded in Britain although, once again, it too has dwindled substantially.

Alexander's point that a roost was often located in the largest rookery may not seem particularly significant, but what undoubtedly resonated with me was his claim that even when there was no active rookery present, one had existed on the same spot at an earlier period. In other words, the roost marked the site of a 'ghost' rookery. Earlier I mentioned the small rookery adjacent to the Buckenham Carrs roost, about 400 metres from the main gathering place, but it was far more intriguing to discover, years after I'd begun, that there was once a rookery in exactly the place where the birds gather. Even more compelling was the revelation that the subroost at Mulberry Carr had also been a rookery thirty years earlier.

★ ★ ★

I'll return to the matter of the ghost rookery as roost site shortly. First I need to explain that not only is there a structured pattern through the seasons to the rooks' dusk and dawn movements, but that each day unfolds according to a comparably strict pattern. This aspect was explored in detail by a Cambridge-educated general practitioner called Franklin Coombs who had settled in Cornwall in the early 1930s. Coombs initiated a study of roosting corvids around his home near the coastal town of Falmouth that is still the *only* long-term investigation of this behaviour in Britain. Eventually he published the results in a series of papers for various journals and finally in a book, *The Crows: A Study of the Corvids of Europe*.

There was a major difference between Coombs' roost scenario and my own. The three roosts he investigated contained more jackdaws than rooks, which was the reverse pattern of Buckenham Carrs. At his main study area there were just 3,600 rooks, compared with 11,000 jackdaws. In the Yare valley I estimate that rooks comprise on average two-thirds of the total. Aside from this discrepancy, the details Coombs described in Cornwall more than half a century earlier bore out what I found in my own Norfolk patch. His main roost was at a place called Enys, a wood just to the north of Falmouth, one part of which — significantly — had once held a rookery that was long vanished.

A point that emerged strongly from Coombs' study was the way in which his

Cornish birds moved with absolute regularity during their winter flights to and from the roost. Over the years he had built up a picture of the routes taken by various subgroups using the Enys location. On a map accompanying one of his papers, the lines of approach were elegantly delineated as radials converging on a central hub. The pattern was consistent. By day the birds dispersed across their parish to feed, often in the vicinity of their own nest colony. Towards late afternoon the group would muster, invariably in the trees of their rookery. Then at a time which Coombs had calculated with impressive precision — an average of 26.8 minutes after sunset in the months of January, February and March — the birds would converge via a fixed flight line on Enys.

The pattern in the Yare is more complicated, possibly because of the sheer size of Buckenham Carrs — at its maximum it's more than twice as large as the Enys roost — and because it includes a far greater percentage of rooks. The birds bound for Buckenham start gathering on their rookeries but then move to a secondary site, a pre-roost gathering, usually closer to their final destination for the night and often in open fields. The location of this assembly is variable and possibly determined by the availability of last-minute feeding opportunities. Finally, from these pre-roost gatherings, where as many as a thousand or several thousand corvids may assemble, they move towards Buckenham Carrs itself.

Once the birds have arrived at fields adjacent to the roost, my observations of roost behaviour converge closely with Coombs' own. His birds, like mine, never flew directly to the roost proper, but would alight in neighbouring fields to wait — an average period that Coombs had calculated at 14.5 minutes — for the assembly of all the subgroups. Only at the moment when all were present would they depart *en masse* for the trees, and I imagined Coombs longing for that final moment, the climax of the whole drama, with the same deep sense of anticipation that I had come to feel. And did he, I often wondered, find it moving and beautiful in its simplicity and predictability? (Alas, I never knew. Coombs died before I even began.)

The one insight Coombs had that affected me most deeply was possibly one to which he would have attached little significance. In a paper in 1961 he suggested that from an average height above the rookery of about 30 metres, 80–90 per cent of the birds in the Enys rook parish could actually see their nighttime destination. I realised that from a similar elevation, and certainly from 100 metres — no great height for a roost-bound rook — the whole Yare-valley population was in direct visual contact with almost all its constituent parts. I experienced a sudden revelation of the unfolding roost process, but as seen from above; as seen by the birds themselves.

It gave me an insight for the first time into how my own circumstance shaped my view of the Yare valley. Like all humans, my eye and brain configured the place according to the most deeply ingrained of reflexes. I saw it not as it is, but as I'm bound by time and place and the condition of my species to see it. The simple impediments imposed on a gravity-bound primate such as ditches, dense bushes, marshy ground — sometimes just the long grass, or the space across open fields between any two fixed points — add a colour wash of emotional and psychological significance. Then there are the gates, barbed-wire fences, no-entry signs and noticeboards of official-dom — the council, the Broads Authority, the powers that be, whatever — with all their political and social implications, that con-strained me to know my place or rather, to know *their* place and my restricted role within it. My sense of the Yare, I realised, was stained entirely with myself.

But then the rooks had their version too. And yet how radically different was this country as seen from above. From horizon to horizon the landscape became at once smaller but freer, more unified and yet more fluid. In the unforgettable phrase of the author of *The Peregrine*, J.A. Baker, it was a world which, 'pouring away behind the moving bird ... flows out from the eye in deltas of piercing colour'. Just like my conditioned geographical sense, the rooks' was one where significance was unevenly distributed across the countryside. It was framed by a network of points loaded with psychological meaning.

The rookery was a key lodestone — a place of high trees, whose engrained familiarity conferred a deep sense of security and comfort. Even the jackdaws, an entirely separate species which have no vested biological interest in the rooks' breeding site, seemed to succumb to its magnetic spell. Why? Perhaps as the light thickens and as these diurnal birds lose their visual grasp on the world, they gather to face the oncoming uncertainties of night at its most secure localities.

The same processes of attachment were at work in the roost proper. The nocturnal sanctuary to which they were oriented every day of their autumn and winter lives was located close to a rookery or even — and here was the real significance of Alexander's insight — where rookeries had *once* existed, precisely because it was these nodes, these crossroads in the landscape, that held the necessary aura of sanctity for corvids to wish to rest there for the night.

Suddenly the Yare valley had become a completely different landscape. It was not mine, it was not even *ours*. It was theirs. I tried to imagine it as they saw it, viewing it through some magical form of heat-imaging equipment. Instead of trees and fields and earth, one saw the place as a sequence of colours. The red areas, the hottest, the most significant spots, were those places loaded with power for rooks, and between them stretched long bright strands, the flight lines that connected a roost with its outlying parish and sketched the routes across the sky. Tunnels of air became causeways as real and palpable as any human path or road, and some of these invisible threads of connection did not just extend through space, but arced though time.

The fourth dimension to crow country was brought home to me once more by those ghost rookeries where the roosts now stand. Mulberry Carr and Buckenham Carrs are not just roosts, they are cultural repositories. To use Richard Dawkins' famous term, they are 'memes' — learned fragments of information that have life independent from the genetic fabric of an individual rook or jackdaw. Knowledge of them is inheritable and handed down from one generation of birds to another. The immediate and original behavioural and psychological links that had once made a rookery also a suitable place for the birds to gather for the night had long since been broken. The rooks and jackdaws which sleep there now are ten, perhaps twenty, generations away from the original birds that once used it as a place to breed. Yet they still feel drawn to the site by inherited patterns of association. And who knows how long the traditions may persist?

Organised natural-historical research — I'm reluctant to call it scientific research because much of it, while of high quality and invaluable as a resource, is mere anecdotal observation — has only existed for three hundred years. Often, reliable data go back only to the mid-nineteenth century. Ageing rook roosts is thus fraught with problems.

Rookeries are, in some ways, better documented. The oldest extant examples that I've seen, with proof of antiquity, include a small colony at Morwenstow church on the north Cornish coast, which dates back to 1855. Another at Trelawne House, near the Cornish village of Pelynt, is 160 years old, and from the written evidence (see also Chapter 17) it was even then the largest in Cornwall. Since there has been a house on the site since Domesday its rookery may well go back centuries. Derek Skilling in Dumfriesshire monitors a site at Gribton, just north of Dumfries, that is known to be 207 years old, while in his *Birds of Dumfriesshire* (1910) Hugh Gladstone lists several rookeries on the Elliock estate at Sanquhar that were said to date back to the 1640s. At least one of the rookeries was in existence until 1963, making it possibly 320 years old.

Roosts feature less often in the written records, and the oldest extant site I know about for which there is some documentation is Braal Castle near Thurso in Caithness. The rookery is said to date to 1775 and its roost may well be equally old. The problems of ageing roosts are perfectly illustrated by the massive congregation first studied by Scottish ecologist Adam Watson in the 1940s at Hatton Castle in Aberdeenshire. The roost is still there, the birds still swarming in as the sun sets, still turning in a great blurred gyre above a place known as 'Craa Wid'. (On the cold clear February night that I visited, it was memorable not just for this sense of history, but also because at the point where the rooks drained into the woods, a full moon steadily arose; not the usual pale glassy lunar face of winter, but a heavily distorted orange-red globe which bulbed up out the Hatton landscape for five minutes before it finally sailed free of the Earth. My companion was so moved he later painted the scene and I have it now on my office wall.) It is inconceivable that the roost at Hatton Castle could have accumulated to 65,000 birds only a few years prior to Watson's study. The house itself dates back to the fifteenth century and my guess is that the roost is also very ancient.

The problems recur in the Yare valley. No one knows when rooks first gathered at Buckenham Carrs; the earliest written records date to the 1970s. (I cherish the fact that among some locals it's believed that the roost is mentioned in the Domesday Book. Sadly, it's not.) Yet if one examines Faden's 1797 map of the county one can see that the wood itself, like Mulberry Carr across the valley, was the only substantial stretch of trees in this section of the valley at the end of the eighteenth century. The age of both woods may well explain their use as roosts (and rookeries) at that time, and the latter's continued existence today. It may just be further wishful thinking on my part, but the neighbouring village is called Rockland St Mary, a name that in the Domesday Book appeared as *Rokelund*, 'Rook Grove'. This was crow country by Saxon times.

★   ★   ★

There is one other profound pleasure which flows from the highly structured nature of roosts and roosting behaviour. When I stand out on the marsh on a winter's evening counting the rooks and jackdaws as they stream overhead, I am simultaneously aware of all the other birds on their parallel trajectories. The setting sun choreographs another great passage across the Yare valley, this one of gulls — black-headed, common, herring, great and lesser black-backeds — which travel on an easterly bearing towards Breydon estuary. Unlike the corvids, the gulls' movement is without an aura of playfulness; it has an almost inexorable, businesslike quality. The distances they travel may be even greater than those covered by the rooks, and by the time they reach the valley they are flying far higher than the corvids. The two bird families never collide or confuse each other's passage, but intersect to create beautiful and momentary geometric patterns across the heavens. In fact at times the gulls are so captivating — their arched white underwings caught in the rose glow from the last rays of sunlight — that I'm lured away from my beloved crows.

On some evenings the silent lines of the gulls are obliterated by a lower swarm, a crackling susurration of starlings, which roost in the reedbeds at Rockland and Strump-shaw. Each night I must also contend with the squalid racket produced by a clumsy honking junta of greylag geese that battle their way to roosts upstream, sometimes in complete darkness. I quickly came to realise that there wasn't just one tradition in the Yare, there were numerous, time-honoured patterns of nightly behaviour, whose paths interconnect across the landscape.

By day it's completely different. The place hosts a sequence of encounters with individual birds in isolated pursuit of their separate lives. It is random, unstructured, without pattern. Its unique unfolding every day is part of the naturalist's pleasure. But dusk brings for me the equal fulfilment of the predictable, the beauty of common purpose. It's a re-enactment of the past, but embodied in the living moment, and I am bewitched by its formal quality, by the sense of an unfolding rite, each part authorising its sequel. At times I have a feeling that the fall of night, the rotation of the Earth, even the orbit of the stars — none of it could take place without the rooks' roost swarm, or the gulls' glinting passage, or the barn owl's moth-like wing beat.

15

The one great unforeseen pleasure resulting from my affair with rooks has been my experience — perhaps, I should really call it my *discovery* — of dusk. Dusk is now embedded in my relationship with the Yare.

I suppose I'd always appreciated the magic. Most birders will tell you that there is an aura to dawn and dusk excursions. Certain crepuscular species emerge only at those moments, and many diurnal birds are most active just after dawn. Rooking is inevitably most intense at either end of the day, but several months into my new calling dusk had acquired the major share of my attention. There is undoubtedly a rational, practical element to the choice. At dawn the birds disperse from the roost in one brief, intense flurry. Fifteen minutes and it's usually all over.

In the evening the process builds slowly to a climax, and there's far more detail to observe, issues to unravel. If I'm honest, the dusk outing also fits far better into the life of a busy father of two with a run-down cottage to repair. Struggling out of bed at three o'clock on a summer's morning is a pretty tough regime. But wandering down the lane and on to the marsh at three on a winter's afternoon feels like restorative therapy, a way of letting go of the day's cares. One whole strand of my natural history is now oriented towards that moment. Dusk has become a purpose in its own right.

My usual goal is to find some spot with an all-encompassing view over the selected field of activity, and then to sit and wait. I think of it as a kind of natural-historical fishing, with a hook and line going both ways: outwards into the landscape for anything that happens to come along, but also inwards into the pool of my unconscious for any striking formula of words rising to the surface in response. In the meantime the heart slows, the breath steadies, the senses attune to the moment, the worries of the world fall away.

Hearing actually improves as dusk assembles itself and I feel I can pick out ever more distant detail, but as the light ebbs so your sight weakens. It's this, strangely, perhaps, that I cherish. Things become less fixed. Commonplace items are blurred and assume unfamiliar characteristics. A perfect example is the lapwings which belt from one side of the valley to the other as darkness falls, to begin feeding under cover of night. Their high *peewit* notes, often the only clue to their passage over the river, have an almost hysterical edge. Suddenly in the blue-black gloom I catch sight of a surging line overhead. A string of about fifty lapwings bulges as it pushes skywards; then once over the Yare the fragments fall in a concave wave back to Earth, their surprisingly small hard silhouettes fading inexorably into the inner recesses of my vision.

On another occasion I caught a flock of wigeon crammed into a dyke so tightly it almost seemed they were afraid of the great space all around. Perhaps 500 birds choked the drain like weed. In the gloaming they were visible merely as a layer of lesser darkness seething on the opaque mass of tranquil water. In truth I heard the commotion more than saw it. When they could finally contain their fears of the darkness no longer, they burst upwards. Lack of light reduced them to something almost inanimate, flakes of tin or sheets of paper riffling skywards after the explosion below.

The slow slippage in one's visual grasp of the environment has other origins in the Yare valley, particularly in autumn and winter, when the waves of sun-warmed air radiating back off the land hit the cold blast of night, to condense as a fine veil above the horizon.

This mist first congeals over the water-filled dykes and then spills in linear shoals out across the fields, gradually back-filling the landscape, winding through the trees, submerging the fixed properties of day in a soft white nebula. Sometimes it lies upon everything in a perfect sheet or encircles the trees, deepening steadily until their tops rise like a free-floating island of vegetation. Occasionally a white lake engulfs me too. But I love most the times when it leaves the river banks just standing proud and isolated above the tide. The bank crown then marks my eerily silent route home to the village, like a dream causeway back to the land of the living.

Not even the power and surging energy of a train can resist the mist. I see the 4.30 from Yarmouth burrowing through the valley like a great subterranean beast that has surfaced. With its eyes shining and a noise that momentarily obliterates the sound of rooks, it succumbs steadily to the place, beetling back into the mist and the silence, and I am left alone once more in possession of the marsh.

I'm under no illusion that this is a place long beaten down by decades of agricultural usage and modification, but the mist and the dusk at least give the sense of a landscape reclaiming its powers of mystery. With their help I can imagine how it once was, dusk bringing a renewed magic even to the most forsaken parts, to the barren arable stretch I call 'abandoned Norfolk'. Here the ghosts emerge with the shadows in exactly the same way and the birds sense the gathering air of tension.

Winter thrushes, shuffling down the hedge in a game of grandmother's footsteps, tumble from their perch as I approach, then weave themselves back among the foliage further along. By the time the moon emerges with its dusty bloom of ice-cloud, the blackbirds' mad metallic *chink-chink-chink* notes rise to near-hysteria. This in turn triggers the pheasants into a louder convulsive *gok-gok-gok* crowing, the notes ricocheting across the landscape like hoarse gunfire. Briefly the world is robed in these glorious night sounds, and the pitter-patter of unseen gamebirds running for their lives through the wood brings a fleeting lupine power to the place. I trudge home in the dark, snapping glassy lids of ice across the puddles on the track, while lights in a distant cottage keep vacant watch like eyes in a Hallowe'en lantern.

★　★　★

The dusk's potential to transform the landscape has for me a deep and countervailing pleasure that results from shedding its power once I get home. Arriving at the house and turning the front-door handle, I sense the cold and the night and the eerie otherworldliness of the tawny owl's song being shaken off like an outer garment. I step inside, I wrestle off my boots, I spot Rachael or Miriam busy at the computer and the orange glow from the coal fire, and it's as if I'm moving not just from one microclimate to another, but between separate psychological realms.

★　★　★

If I had to pick a precise moment in the great cycle of dusks then I would choose late summer/early autumn as my favourite. The fields on the marsh give rise to a great bed of Yorkshire fog, a grass species that turns steadily over June and July from a horizon of soda-cream white to a soft purple then back to a desiccated tone that's almost exactly the same colour as a lioness' flanks. Yorkshire fog seldom grabs the attention. Summer seems to lie upon it as on a great couch, while its muted tones appeal to a deeper layer of consciousness and each year's fresh crop is laden with half-buried memories from all the summers I've ever known.

The sounds in that portion of the year appeal in exactly the same way to a subliminal realm rather than to one's active mental processes. Late summer is the time when most birds stop singing and they leave that vast domain of silence to one or two persistent voices, such as the wood pigeon's. It's a deep hoarse crooning, soporific in its effect and easy to overlook, which is strange because in modern Britain it's now nearly ubiquitous and as I walk down the summer lanes one sleepy song unconsciously delivers me to the territory of a neighbour.

The pigeons' oboe-like notes complement another secret chorus of our summer dreams, the *Orthoptera*, the grasshoppers. In the early part of the season the key sound is the sustained fifteen-second pulse of the common green grasshopper. But within a matter of weeks that prolonged stridulation is replaced by the brief chirp of the field grasshoppers. Their one- or two-second purr often counterpoints with a close neighbour, so that they seem to sing in tandem, like tiny bellows, in and out. Field grasshoppers can be heard long after nightfall and late into the year, sometimes even in November. It may seem illogical when written down, but I feel this song is so small and dry, it deepens the silence of late summer.

I love this moment. The rooks are sometimes just a sideshow to these rooking excursions. By late June the rookery and its inhabitants have vanished into the season's vast dark chlorophyll shadows, and the sub-roost in Mulberry Carr attracts no more than a few hundred heavily moulted birds, some so ragged it's extraordinary they can fly at all. I go down to count to keep my hand in, but I'm easily distracted: by the whine of chironomid midges choiring down the dykes in linear clouds; or the staccato gunning of magpies *en famille*; or the convulsive *ker-chink* notes of swallows that are usually the tell-tale sign of a hobby or sparrow-hawk spearing over the fields.

At times even the cattle lure me away from the birds. By late summer the livestock numbers on the marsh are at their greatest. Often they're young black bullocks filled with the spirit of youth or goaded by the Yare's numerous horse-flies. They surround any human intruder, especially at dusk, with a perpetual comedic attention. If I stand to watch the rooks, leaning my binoculars on one of the five-bar gates, they instantly mass towards me, inadvertently blocking the view. And if they're cut off from immediate contact by a water-filled dyke, they canter away in frustration, then bank round in a sweeping arc, hoofs pounding, to line up on the opposite shore in perfect formation. They snort and fling their heads up and down to mark their annoyance.

It's deeply unnerving to feel the physical sensation of their weight and power vibrating through the ground and I thank God for the deep water that separates us, only to break into audible laughter at the sight of their large plastic yellow ear-tags flapping in sync, the beasts coughing like bronchitic old men. In a final note of bathos one will hose the ground with a great jet of piss. Others catch the urge, and all start quietly to munch and ruminate, long strands of vegetation dangling from their muzzles, as if the act of enquiry held them for a moment in suspended animation.

Yet the cattle can also create a vastly different mood. When the mist steals out of the dykes at twilight and winds gradually around them, it appears less that this shroud rises to engulf the cows than that the black beasts themselves are emerging from the Earth. The animals you presumed to know, with their comic threads of spittle and their comforting sweet straw smell, are now mysterious and new like giants resurrected in a primordial landscape.

★   ★   ★

There is another aspect to the failing light which makes rooking at dusk so satisfying. As I said earlier, the birds' behaviour builds to an obvious climax. However there's an inverted relationship between the interest value of what's unfolding and your ability to see it. And matters are at their most compelling at the point when they're virtually invisible. It adds a layer of tension to the whole proceedings. Occasionally, in certain circumstances, the entire thing is a one-shot deal. You either achieve your end, or you have to wait twenty-four hours to try again. Sometimes, as at Dunscore in Dumfriesshire, there are no second chances.

Here are two diary accounts of separate dusk experiences. The first also occurred in Dumfriesshire on 12 January 2005. I was searching for another old roost of 10,000 birds identified in the 1971 paper that had led me to Dunscore. I wanted to discover if it too was still in existence. It was listed as a site called 'Halluchs, Lochmaben'. Even that was problematic. A forage through the literature on local place names at Dumfries library eventually revealed that the locality had been rechristened on recent maps as Halleaths, a hamlet just north-east of Lochmaben.

Scanned from Halleaths but nothing except far distant birds tracking in small numbers on consistent north-north-west bearing across the loch, but not turning east to the old 1971 site where I stood. I drove two miles north to village of Templand in order to see where they were going. No sign.

Worse, I was thrown a total red herring by the presence of a flock of c. 200 birds over a rookery site near Templand. I thought this might be the replacement roost for Halleaths. So I stood waiting, hoping, ten, fifteen, twenty minutes. As birds started to leave in twos and threes, also heading west, it eventually dawned on me: the flock was simply reconnecting with its rookery before the roost. Come nightfall all would be gone. And I'd be left alone in the dark, unable to follow.

It was pretty dark already. But the road didn't go where the birds were heading. I was pushed north and they were going west. So I drove out of Templand until it did a full loop around, and by the time I was looking south-east — i.e. back towards the point where I had started off, at the Halleaths end of Lochmaben — I'd totally lost them.

Nothing was moving at all. It was night now. But something made me stop and suddenly there they were, c. 2000 birds in a field just east of an unnamed plantation c. 1.5 miles north-east of Lochmaben. They were sat in one dense huddle, completely silent. A great black slab of cloud sheared through the last wedge of ice-blue light and in minutes the darkness collapsed upon us. Then in sheeting rain the birds rose.

It was fortunate that several cars, headlights blazing, were running towards me and at right angles to the ragged lines of rooks and jackdaws. As the corvids rose gradually above the skyline, they cut a clear silhouette through the falling rain. It was magical: a closing arc of white light tunnelling towards me, the inky shadows through a lesser darkness and across everything in brilliant points the diamond glint of the rain. Within a minute the flock of 2000 had vanished completely.

One of the largest holes in my geographical grasp of the Buckenham gathering was the whereabouts of its neighbouring roost some-where down the Yare/Waveney valley. I'd known of its existence since the winter of

2002, when I was surprised one evening to see birds gathered in a pre-roost flock near the hamlet of Thorpe depart in two separate directions. Some had headed west for Buckenham, but from the foreshortened perspective of the valley floor it appeared as if the others had headed in more or less the opposite direction — east-north-east, towards the village of Somerleyton, in Suffolk.

'Somerleyton' served as its working title, but during the intervening years the exact location of this roost remained a mystery. Other priorities always stopped me from looking for it, yet I knew that it exerted a fluctuating gravitational hold over rooks breeding in that section of the valley. I was also tantalised by a reference in Claud Ticehurst's *A History of the Birds of Suffolk* (1932), which read: 'Somewhere beyond Beccles there is a roost which I have not located, but which draws all the Rooks from as far off as Lowestoft, and the evening flight up the Waveney marshes is a very regular event.' I wondered if his unknown roost and mine were one and the same. Finally, on 18 December 2005, I determined to sort it out. My notes for the evening read:

Finally found the other 'Yare' roost after four years. Took some doing. I drove to the bridge over the New Cut at about 3 o'clock and looked south towards Haddiscoe and Thorpe. But there was no movement of birds from those rookeries to Somerleyton. Instead all the birds I could see were heading west towards Buckenham.

At 3.30 I drove down to Somerleyton railway station itself, which is right on the northern edge of the lower Waveney valley. I was pretty shocked to discover a rookery I didn't even know existed, just west of the station approach road. Since the birds were breeding so close to where I assumed the other roost was, I decided to keep a watch over them. Surely they'd lead me to it?

I went out on to the fields where I could look back north towards the rookery and get a wider overview. However I must have got distracted, scanning across the marsh to the south, because I turned round and suddenly they'd all completely vanished. Since they weren't visible heading west, I knew they must have gone east. I rushed back to the car and checked the map to see how I could follow them. The road ran along the edge of the Waveney valley, away from Somerleyton, so I took it

— little more than a dirt track — until I dared risk the car no further.

I assumed from my memory of where the birds had flown last time that I was close to the roost. I got out and jogged down the track running parallel with the valley's northern edge. I was cut off from the full panorama across the marsh by a thin belt of trees along a steepish slope, but I thought I'd come back upon them at any minute. Eventually however the track emerged at a clearing with views over the flats and there was no sign of anything. I was beginning to panic. Where the hell had they gone? I kept going, maintaining a bearing of roughly due east.

The path was hard ridged mud thick with ice and huge ice-glazed puddles that smashed up with every step. It was really rough. The fast pace and my down jacket made me increasingly hot. Expanding patches of damp glued the shirt to my back and real pain was spreading across my shins from the stress of negotiating such a rutted track. I unzipped the jacket but it didn't really have much effect and my binoculars were completely steamed over.

Luckily I got a fix on c. 70 birds, some

of which had just come in from the south. Through a fog of condensation I could see them going down on a distant belt of trees and set out to reach them before they went to the roost proper. However the track just seemed to run away and parallel to the line of trees the birds were in. I was cut off by several thick hedges and just had to keep going.

One intriguing discovery was a flock of several hundred pink-footed geese coming off the lower Waveney marshes, presumably from around Oulton. They circled repeatedly over the track, calling all the while with those typical short dog-like notes. Eventually I could see a handful land in a field north of the track but the majority were spooked either by my bright red jacket, or the woman and her two dogs that I met coming the other way.

The track eventually reached a junction and I could see *c.* 200-300 j'daws and rooks on the treetops some way off. I decided that I'd come so far I should finish the business. So I set off again — now extremely overheated — straight across the snow-covered fields. It was virtually dark and I was in unknown territory. I was really worried about getting lost, there was no sign of an imminent moon, and I carefully checked my route so I could retrace it on the return. I crossed one field, then another and I realised I was getting close.

Then came one of those moments that so justified all my efforts. I was scanning the few hundred birds (largely j'daws) in the trees when I suddenly noticed what looked like about 1000 rooks sitting quietly in a snow-covered field, a silent black pool all the more striking for its utterly silent white matrix. I dashed across the last field intending to get a rough sense of total numbers when they flew. Several thousand birds swirled upwards, threading their way through that typical deep roar of bass notes which rooks always make in flight. Fulfilment complete.

I could ease my pace on the way home, but only the latent glow of the snow-covered landscape made navigation possible. I was most surprised on the return to find that the 'two-minute' section closest to the car, where I'd kept parallel with the valley floor, was about half a mile in length. It took me more than ten minutes to cover this stretch and I was thoroughly relieved finally to reach the vehicle. Once in the light I could barely believe how much ground I'd covered. It took careful examination of the map to confirm that the roost site was nowhere near Somerleyton. It was a good four-mile round walk from the car, a place called Flixton Carr, that was nearer to the outskirts of Lowestoft, and probably the site for all the birds in the Lowestoft area. At last. One more small mystery plucked from the darkness.

16

I can date very precisely my breakthrough in understanding the *why* of rook roosts, as opposed to the *what*. It was the moment of dusk on 17 September 2004. At the time, it didn't feel like a breakthrough at all. In fact, the complete reverse. Almost from the moment I arrived on the marsh by Mulberry Carr and raised my binoculars to watch the birds coming in for the evening, I was thrown into confusion.

Normally I log them in my notebook as they appear, listing the size of each individual flock, its time of arrival and the cumulative total. But after just six separate entries — 222 birds — I gave up. Rooks and jackdaws were sweeping into the fields adjacent to Mulberry Carr on a high change-laced wind. There was no slow, orderly, incremental build-up in numbers. They came in widely spaced drifts like showers of black blossom, their movements wild and playful, the calls incessant. The mood was electric, exhilarating. It felt as if the change of seasons was happening before my very eyes and, in a sense, it was. I didn't try to make notes. It was too uncontrollable, too wild to contain. I simply stood back and watched.

After the birds arrived they appeared to go to land in the fields furthest from the Mulberry Carr roost trees. Then they would progressively loop up over their nearest neighbours and drop down again in the field so that they could tease out for as long as possible this steady drift towards their nightly spot. There was something magical about the way the flock constantly reconfigured. A soft undertow of pale pink light caught the gloss of their wings and when a group rose they were shown up against the deeper matt darkness of the woods as a shiver of pale flakes.

By 7.15 p.m. it all seemed to be ending with a whimper rather than the bang I'd anticipated. The energy of that extraordinary evening was steadily drained. Even the dense mass of black bullocks, which had seemed to share the corvids' earlier mood of exhilaration, scattered as indifferent islands of darkness across the fields. But then half the total of the gathered flock, possibly 1,500-2,000 birds, rose as one and instead of heading for the sanctuary of Mulberry Carr, as I had watched them do on every evening throughout that summer and early autumn, they split in two. A breakaway group instantly streamed off north away from their roost in a long thin pipe across the sky, back towards Buckenham. The main flock then rose and gyred above Mulberry Carr, wildly agitated by the sudden rupture in their unity. I too felt enmeshed in the confusion, not knowing which way to look. But the breakaway party rotated so violently over the fields around Buckenham Carrs, the great wing-scape passing in and out of view as its angle changed in relation to me, that I felt compelled to follow and I dashed along the bank to get a better view. At its most dramatic I could see a great rainbow arc of black birds across the entire valley, its distal ends melting into two completely separate roosts. Between was a community in flux, oscillating wildly between the critical fixtures in their social life.

*   *   *

I had just witnessed for the first time the exact moment when the autumn roost at Mulberry Carr broke down and the birds began their reversion to the Buckenham site. I now appreciate that it's an annual event, falling between the first and third weeks of September. By October all sense of confusion is gone. Mulberry Carr is deserted. Buckenham has become the sole fixture in their daily lives. I may now have grown accustomed to the brief chaos that the transfer inspires, but at the time it made a profound impression.

By sheer coincidence I'd been reading a book by the environmentalist Eric Hoyt entitled *The Earth Dwellers*. It's an excellent work on ants and it seemed almost uncanny that on the night before my encounter with the Mulberry-Buckenham transfer I'd read a passage about the formation of new colonies in *Eciton* army ants, a group native to Latin America.

The social life of an ant colony revolves around its queen, who is the mother of all its members — the workers, the male offspring essential to the process of reproduction, and all the future queens — sometimes as many as 20 million in total. After the queen has laid eggs that develop into the new virgin queens, more and more of the workers transfer allegiance from their mother to their sisters. When the new queens finally make a bid to establish their own separate group, deep confusion ensues. The colony, which had previously functioned like a well-oiled machine (a 'super-organism', according to formicologists, a word that suggests the way the millions of separate parts operate like one large entity), breaks down entirely.

According to Hoyt, only two queens,

usually the first hatched, manage to establish fresh colonies. The existing queen, however, the original mother of them all, will also make a bid to maintain half the colony with her. But if she is too old, if her potency is diminished and she is unable to command loyalty through the pheromones, the chemical signals, that she gives off, then her formerly loyal workers will abandon her, and her daughters will command the newly divided colony. Hoyt describes the aftermath of this final rupture:

> For two days . . . the virgin army ant queens with their workers begin to establish their independence. Their raids are rather weak and their new life still tenuous. On the morning of the second day, the virgin colonies are still connected by a two-ant trail of workers moving in either direction. The traffic, much less than the previous day and growing thinner by the hour, is composed of confused workers still unsure about their allegiance. By mid-morning it disappears . . . all have gone with one or the other.

In twenty-four hours I'd been offered two separate visions of deep confusion in nature.

It seemed to subvert some fundamental expectation. I'd come to assume that while humans might be susceptible to conflicting impulses, other species were not. The 'nature' out there was neat and ordered. It operated according to rules, predictable and free from turmoil. Roosting rooks shouldn't behave like that. They were a finely tuned mechanism, functioning as I'd come to expect from reading Franklin Coombs on his roost at Enys in Cornwall. His birds left their rookery at a precise moment, they arrived at the roost with equal exactitude and then they flew to the roost trees proper, according to Coombs, an average of 14.5 minutes later.

In truth, my rooks had never behaved with quite the same regularity. (There may be good reasons for the differences between my roost observations and Coombs', which I'll come to later.) While there may be small discrepancies, the whole thing had often suggested to me the formal qualities of a ritual. The detail might vary a little, but the basic facts were the same. The realisation that an organism as apparently automaton-like as an ant could encounter moments of deep crisis and uncertainty opened up new possibilities. My experience of the rooks that night then threw the subject wide open. Awareness that there could be confusion in the *what* of rook roosts set up a lateral process. Maybe the *why* was also confused? And if not confused, then at least complicated. Ideas started to take shape.

★   ★   ★

One of the most surprising things about all the various studies on rook roosts is how few authors, especially prior to the 1970s, ever asked *why* they form. It was almost as if the answer was so obvious that the question didn't even need to be posed. Yet the very first British author on the subject did ask. Edgar Harper studied rook roosts in the Leeds area and published a paper in 1904 in a volume of the short-lived *Bradford Scientific Journal* (as far as I'm aware it's the earliest specific study on the subject), and he concluded that the birds were seeking 'shelter and safety'.

I suspect that this was the assumption of all the other observers who never directly tackled the issue, including the most significant, such as Wilfred Alexander and Franklin Coombs. It occurs to me that any layperson must feel that by reflecting on their own behaviour they gain insight into the roosting habits of a diurnal social species like ourselves, or even the rook. To bolt the door, stoke up the fire and draw the chairs in a closer circle around the television may be a quintessentially modern response to nightfall, but the actions reflect our ancient human urge for warmth, security and the re-establishment of shared bonds, which has persisted since we lived in caves. Other primates such as gorillas and chimps make equally elaborate arrangements, including the construction of special leafy nests in which to bed down, while baboons occasionally drop inter-troop rivalries and band together if secure sleeping sites are at a premium.

Security, in various forms, has long been associated with flocking behaviour. One obvious benefit is the presence of all those extra eyes keeping watch so that a predator can be detected whatever its line of approach. Another advantage is the confusion generated by the protean swirls of an evading flock. If you watch a sparrowhawk steam into a roost of starlings, you'll see the birds morph into a single entity — a 'super-organism', perhaps — pulsing and twisting like wood smoke in an autumn wind. The mesmerising impact it has on the human observer is thought to be an analogue of the deep bewilderment engendered in the hunting hawk. A third dividend is the dilution of risk enjoyed by each flock member: in a large group, there is a smaller chance that any individual will become the predator's victim.

The flip-side to predator detection and evasion is the inherent drawback of presenting to any bird of prey a predictable, twice-daily source of ready protein. In fact raptors are positively drawn to roosts. My own observations suggest that rooks and jackdaws are alive to this risk. Birds approaching the roost site sometimes descend upon the area in a wild downward tumbling flight, performing a series of abrupt switch-back twists and swerves. Edgar Harper also noted it and suggested that 'anyone who has not witnessed these aerial evolutions can obtain an excellent idea of them by cutting an outline of a bird with outstretched wings in paper, and dropping it from a fairly good height'.

If there were any lurking bird of prey then it strikes me that the simultaneous downward trajectory of the rooks would be an excellent pre-emptive response, confusing and challenging the predator. It's known technically as 'whiffling' and it may be a parallel to the 'stotting' or 'pronking' display of many African antelopes. This is a highly conspicuous leaping action performed by alarmed antelopes to advertise potential danger to fellow herd members. To a predator like a lion, stotting is thought to signal that pursuit would be hopeless. The stotting individual is an antelope in the prime of physical fitness. Whiffling may make the same posturing statement. A bird capable of such a wild careening plunge to Earth is not going to make an easy catch.

An interesting side issue of whiffling is that it's performed not just by rooks, but also by really large roosting species such as cormorants and geese. It is hard now to imagine that it has an active anti-predator function for these birds, because there are so few — if any — predators large enough to take a cormorant or pink-footed goose in full flight. What it may conjure up, however, is that ancient moment when whiffling did have genuine survival value. What one should perhaps try to see is the ghost impression of a roost-bound goose snatched in midair by a hunting white-tailed or golden eagle. In short, this imagined tableau is the genesis for the whiffling reflex present still in geese and cormorants. Humans may have reduced eagle numbers to render the action largely superfluous, but evolution hasn't eliminated the anti-predator strategy from goose genes. In exactly the same way, the great landscape historian Oliver Rackham speculates on whether the coppicing reflex shown by cut deciduous trees was originally a means of coping with the destructive impact of elephants. Although the latter no longer bulldoze through the European landscape, even now our trees retain their anti-pachyderm strategy for regrowing once knocked down.

I also speculate whether much the same thing obtains in rooks. I've only once seen a peregrine make a half-hearted pass at jackdaws on Anglesey, and never seen a successful attack by any raptor during the many hundreds of occasions I've watched corvid roosts. There is very little danger to the current British roosting flock, but perhaps the birds retain their whiffling just in case, as a trump card.

One thing we know for definite is that the fear of predators cannot be the only, or the primary, motor driving roost behaviour. The threat from birds of prey to a corvid roost flock never varies much beyond the minimal whatever the season, yet roosting behaviour itself changes vastly. In late July there may be no more than a few hundred birds in a summer / autumn congregation like Mulberry Carr. By late February there can be anything up to 40,000 at Buckenham. Clearly some other mechanism is at work to propel that process of concentration.

Given the seasonal fluctuation, the other

strand of the security argument — protection from bad weather and low temperature — would seem a possible trigger. In some species it is known to be the central benefit of roosting. The case is well illustrated by an intensely anti-social species like the wren, whose gatherings only occur during periods of intense cold. Wrens temporarily abandon their hermit's lifestyle and muster towards dusk in a secure cranny or hole, although the mechanism that actually shapes the otherwise atypical behaviour has never been pinpointed. One of the most striking examples involved ninety-six wrens cloistered in the eaves of a Gloucestershire roof during the arctic winter of 1979.

Another unusual roost involved sixty Norfolk birds squeezed inside a nestbox during a period of sharp frost in February 1969. Their tiny lodgement provided a mere 38 cubic centimetres per wren and in the morning it took them at least twenty minutes to extricate themselves from the box-of-figs press of bodies. At least one asphyxiated individual was found dead at the bottom. Yet the benefits of snuggling together are perfectly demonstrated by the impact of the big winter freeze of 1963, when four-fifths of Britain's 20 million wrens are thought to have perished.

Despite its prominent appendage, the long-tailed tit has a smaller body mass than the wren and is another species that habitually forms communal roosts. At nightfall the birds squeeze together in a line along the perch and look like a series of pingpong balls threaded on a horizontal cord. It is thought that their need to pass the long northern winter night in a down-cloaked huddle is a key factor in their intensely social lifestyle, including a collaborative form of chick-rearing, in which adult long-tailed tits often aid their siblings to rear the next generation of roost-forming nephews and nieces.

Pied wagtails provide parallel evidence that enhanced insulation is an important element in the roost-forming habit. Pairs of wagtails normally pass their days in a fiercely maintained territory but, together with migrants and young birds, they may also create a distinctive version of the night collective. Their roosts are invariably sited in places offering protection from the elements, such as the interior of greenhouses or factories. One industrial site in Preston even came with its own central heating: the birds spent the night perched on lagged hot-water pipes. The inner city, with its distinctly warmer microclimate, offers a whole suite of valuable roosting opportunities. One pictur-esque example occurred in the heart of Norwich where the birds assembled in a line of trees on the main shopping street. During late December evenings, when the bare branches were bedecked with festive lights, the neon-illuminated wagtails looked like a unique kind of Christmas decoration.

Rook roosts are notable for being located in places — private estates or lands without public access — that carry very small risk of physical disturbance. Most of the sites located around Leeds by Edgar Harper, not to mention Buckenham, Flixton and Mulberry Carr, are all good examples. The value of such secure locations is obvious. Should roosting birds ever be flushed, the energy expenditure inflicted by a hazardous night-time flight, especially in low temperatures, might be severe. At undisturbed sites they will never or hardly ever be roused from their slumbers.

It is equally striking that most large roosts (but not all: for instance, Outtle Well near Wigtown in 1971) include a component of evergreen coverage in the wood. It was as true of Coombs' Enys site as it is of Buckenham Carrs. The most compelling proof I've had of the importance of conifers was the time we wandered through the woods at Hatton Castle, one-time champion of Britain's corvid congregations. My companion on the occasion was my friend Tim Dee. We'd travelled to Scotland to record the Hatton site and to interview its owner for a radio programme on the rook's year.

On the second night of our visit we were confronted with an Aberdeenshire landscape blanketed in snow, the crisp, tobogganing snow you recall from childhood. The deep Hatton woods, with their intricate contours of spruce, larch, pine and beech, had dissolved into a binary world of black tree trunks spiring into an enfolded whiteness. Everything else was snow-softened shadow. Even the silence came with its snow muffler. Tim wandered through the drifts, microphone high above his head, absorbed in his self-appointed task to capture its soundscape. The other trees were empty of birds, but the canopy of each conifer had become a small cavern, utterly dark, a refuge for some of the thousands of Hatton jackdaws. The snow smothered the usual bounce and resonance contained in the jackdaws' notes. Instead what came down to us from the dark canopy was a quietly modulated jabbering, like anxious souls in whispered conclave. To us those tall conifers in that snow were magical; for the birds they were possibly a matter of life and death.

There is little doubt that rooks choose

often to roost inside the heart of woods which, as we know, is an atypical habitat for a traditionally steppe species, if not for its perpetual bedfellow the jackdaw. However, the rook chooses this exceptional site because it provides it with optimum shelter. Other studies have shown that during high wind the corvids tend to congregate on a wood's leeward side to increase the protective impact.

Rooks and jackdaws pass the night in pairs on the roost perch. They don't huddle in a compressed line like the long-tailed tits, which is what you might expect if heat retention were the key function of roosts. Nor do they choose sites composed entirely of conifers, which they would prefer if thermal insulation were paramount. Within a short distance of Buckenham Carrs there are such evergreen sites, but they hold no attraction for the present corvid population. A final but central obstacle to the idea that the rook/jackdaw roost is primarily an issue of shelter is that the roosting habit functions in July, albeit to a lesser extent, as well as in January.

* * *

This brings us to the other major theory postulated to explain roost behaviour in many species of bird. It's based on their value as information centres. The idea was most fully explored in a 1973 paper entitled 'The Importance of Certain Assemblages of Birds as 'Information Centres' for Food-finding', by P. Ward and A. Zahavi. Its authors proposed that members of a flock that had been unsuccessful while feeding earlier in the day responded positively to the behaviour of other well-fed roost attendants. Instead of flying out again to search at random the following morning, the hungry birds would follow the successful neighbours from the roost to learn the whereabouts of the latter's food source and to share it. Ward and Zahavi discussed their theory largely in the context of white and pied wagtail, which the second author had studied in Israel and Britain, but also in the light of Ward's studies of an Africa finch called the red-billed quelea. The quelea is notable for being the most abundant bird in the world and for forming massive swarms sometimes numbering millions of individuals, behaviour that has earned it a secondary name as the 'avian locust'.

Aspects of the theory were subsequently explored in the context of a close rook relative, the northern raven. In the 1980s the American zoologist, Bernd Heinrich, focused on one intriguing element in the social behaviour of wintering raven flocks in Maine, New England. A major source of food for these scavenging birds is the carcasses of large mammals. Heinrich was puzzled by the fact that some ravens, having discovered dead deer or other valuable sources of meat, seemed to call to fellow ravens with a special 'yelling' note, as if they wanted to rally the others to their food find. To Heinrich, who described the studies in his book, *Ravens in Winter*, it appeared that the birds were exhibiting behaviour that subverted a basic tenet of natural selection. Rather than keeping the discovery to themselves and securing their own survival by exclusive access to the meat, the ravens appeared to be beckoning fellow birds to share the bounty.

In a brilliant piece of wildlife detective work, Heinrich eventually unravelled what lay behind the apparent altruism. The yelling individuals were juveniles or non-breeding wanderers, and the purpose of the calls was to recruit others after a carcass had been found. In areas where ravens breed the countryside is parcelled up into fiercely defended territories, each occupied by a resident pair. The purpose of the recruitment was to build up a critical mass of fellow non-resident birds to overwhelm the defences of a dominant couple that would otherwise monopolise access to the carcass. While individual intruders could be chased away, flocks could not. The yelling calls therefore helped to bypass the resident pair and ensure collective access to the meat.

Heinrich also uncovered the fact that much of the recruitment took place in roosts where immature and non-territory-holding birds gathered for the night (resident pairs, by contrast, roost alone in the sanctity of their territory). How this precise mechanism worked wasn't something he unravelled in the course of his book. However, a series of elegant experiments conducted by a trio of British biologists — Jonathan Wright, Richard Stone and Nigel Brown — showed precisely how a roost could function as a recruitment centre. Their work was conducted at Newborough Warren on Anglesey, in north Wales, which had the largest raven roost in Europe throughout the 1990s. At its height in January 1997 the authors counted around 1,900 birds.

Ravens still gather in stands of predominantly Corsican pine along a ridge of Pre-Cambrian rock that finally pushes out beyond Newborough's forest on to the beach, in a curving dragon's tail of black crags called Ynys Llanddwyn. On the November evening in 2003 when we went to witness something of this impressive gathering, my friend Tony Hare and I (not forgetting Tony's five-year-old son, my godson, Adam, who has been known ever after as 'raven boy') counted 129 birds coming in parties of up to seven at a time. We could only census birds recruited from a small north-westerly arc of Anglesey itself, but at its height the roost drew ravens from a full 360-degree catchment area, including mainland Wales. One of our most memorable sightings occurred on the following cold crisp dawn. Venus was just fading from the heavens above Caernarfon's skyline when seven ravens beat a direct path out of Newborough, across the Menai Straits and up towards Snowdonia's towering hills beyond.

The reason why the Newborough roost recruited birds from such distances was well illustrated when Wright and his colleagues provided the ravens with a regular food supply. Twenty-six sheep carcasses that they put out for the birds were carefully doctored using 500 colour-coded plastic fishing beads. During the night at the roost, ravens disgorge pellets containing the indigestible parts of their day's food intake. By gathering and noting the presence of beads in these cast pellets the authors were able to demonstrate which raven first found the carcass and the whereabouts in the roost of any subsequent birds whose pellets contained plastic beads. They showed that there was a direct relationship between the ravens' consumption of the bead-impregnated food and their place in the roost. The beads revealed that information about the location of the carcass moved outwards from the first bird to its roost neighbour and then to others until the sheep was completely consumed.

⋆　⋆　⋆

The experiments by Wright and his colleagues demonstrate incontrovertibly that roosts function as information centres for ravens. The question is, does the same apply to the raven's close relatives? The matter is much more difficult to prove in rooks and jackdaws because these two corvids don't generally feed on such highly concentrated food sources. Although rooks, like ravens, produce cast pellets of indigestible remains, how could one secrete plastic pellets in subsoil invertebrates? No one has yet shown that rook/jackdaw roosts function in the same way.

Yet the circumstantial evidence indicates that they do. One of the strongest clues is the close relationship between roost size and day length. Roosting behaviour is at its loosest when there are eighteen or more hours of daylight each day. It gradually increases thereafter, and it's notable that the transfer from the Mulberry summer/autumn roost to the main winter Buckenham site takes place in mid-September. On 25–26 September dawn and dusk (at latitude 52 degrees north) are almost exactly twelve hours apart.

My own *ad hoc* examination of the impact of light confirms its critical role in roost timings. In January 2006 I looked at the birds' departure from the roost in different light conditions. Just three sets of data indicate the impact. The trigger for a mass exodus was the moment that my camera registered a shutter speed of one quarter of a second (on 4.2 F aperture, with a 100 ASA rated film) in the northern sky. Until the light reached that level in some area of the sky, often towards the east, no birds left the roost. On 9 January the departure took place at 7.25. Just two days later — a morning of thick low cloud — not a bird stirred until 7.57. And by 21 January, a dawn of brilliant ice-blue light, thousands were streaming from the roost at 7.16. One needs to bear in mind that sunrise is actually ten minutes earlier on the 21st than on 9 January. So the times of departure for those two dates, respectively

7.25 and 7.16, correlate to within a few seconds. The striking anomaly is the departure time on that dull dreary 11 January. The birds stayed more than thirty minutes longer in the roost because of the poor light.

In the nine-week window of December-January, therefore, one has the following background circumstances. Corvid roost concentration is at its maximum, and my guess is that the entire rook/jackdaw population of Norfolk (as well as parts of northern Suffolk) — somewhere between 80,000 and a quarter of a million birds — passes the night in about a dozen relatively small areas of woodland. That same period is exactly the time when daylight is in shortest supply. The birds have a maximum of eight hours to find sufficient food to see them through the longest period of darkness. On dull days there is a double deficit because the birds leave the roost later *and* return earlier. On some really foggy December afternoons I've found that all normal feeding activity ceases by about 14.00. It is likely that in late December, on a day with complete dawn-to-dusk cloud cover, they have just six hours to fuel up for a fast of eighteen hours. This is also the period when average temperatures are lowest, and probably the time when the landscape is most depleted of resources. Imagine that stressed situation continuing night after night, day after day. If ever there was an occasion when food information would be at a premium, it is in this period.

While I acknowledge that it is equally circumstantial, I think I have other evidence to support the idea of information exchange. It arises from the very recruitment and dispersal processes at the Buckenham roost. Unfortunately my details are flatly contradicted by the data contained in the paper by Franklin Coombs on his Enys site in Cornwall. His birds, with clockwork regularity, visited the rookery each evening before flying to their roost and, then, in a reverse pattern, returned to the rookery on leaving the roost at dawn. Such automatic reflex movements appear to leave no scope for the roost to serve as an information centre, because birds would hardly have time to go to the rookery first if they were following other knowledgeable individuals or groups to feeding areas. In other words, the roost-as-information-centre would require the pattern of arrival and departure to be flexible and unpredictable, in accordance with the random location and availability of rich food sources.

That is precisely what I find in the height of winter at Buckenham. Birds don't always visit the rookery at dawn. That behaviour is highly variable. Some days they do, some they don't. Equally, flight lines to the roost in the evening differ enormously. On one very notable occasion, I stood on the south bank of the Yare expecting the usual north-flowing lines of thousands of corvids into Buckenham from further south. Yet on the night hardly a bird came from that direction. Almost all of them arrived from the west, from the direction of Norwich.

The occasionally substantial variation in the pattern of flight lines to and from Buckenham need not necessarily be a blanket negation of Coombs' findings. The background climatic and feeding circumstances may not always require rooks to exploit the information-exchange possibilities of a roost. It could be a latent advantage, like an insurance policy, to be activated if things go wrong. But if there is sufficient food immediately around the rookery, then resident birds might restrict their feeding area to its vicinity. They know it intimately and are able to exploit its resources precisely because of their familiarity. That situation may continue for months, even possibly years.

Although it may seem harsh, I wonder also if there could have been another factor at work in Coombs' findings. Remember he never actually asked *why* the birds gather in roosts. He was not trying to solve any problem. The absence of any enquiry as to purpose may have helped shape his preconceptions about what roosts were and how they operated. I know from my own experience that one tends to look for data that confirm a hunch or theory. When the information contradicts the thesis, or just simply leaves you in a state of confusion, there is a tendency to want to ignore it. Coombs was only interested in the *what*, the temporal and geographical structure of roosts. He may have disregarded anomalies that seemed like meaningless variations on the clear structures he thought he'd already established.

The Enys roost's location in Cornwall may itself be a final factor in explaining the notable difference between our findings. His birds were largely jackdaws and resident rooks and there seemed to have been little variation in annual maxima. Yet since 2001 in the Yare valley I have recorded a yearly maximum total that has fluctuated between about 10,000 and as many as 40,000 birds. One key difference is the presence of non-resident rooks and jackdaws from Europe. Northern continental rooks are migrants. They leave regions that become routinely snow-covered or ice-bound for warmer wintering grounds to the west and south. Eastern England and Scotland receive varying numbers of these European birds, but Cornwall seldom if ever does. Therefore the Yare roost may well contain a significant and changing percentage of visitors. And these are precisely the birds least likely to have local information on prime feeding areas, so the roost's ability to serve as an information centre might be critical to their winter survival.

It raises the possibility that roosts operate in different ways for different members of them. For non-resident naïve individuals the primary value might lie in following resident birds out to otherwise unknown feeding sites. The resident populations may thus enjoy a dominant status in the roost and occupy more central locations in the trees. They can monopolise the best perches for thermal protection or defence against predators. The naïve non-residents, on the other hand, may gain access to food information but may roost at the margins and provide a protective buffer around their higher-status neighbours.

There is supportive evidence for the roost's multiple purpose in a study on the structured arrangement of the birds on the branches at night. Ian Swingland found that the dominant older rooks acquire the higher, more sheltered spots in the trees, while young birds are forced to the chillier 'basement' positions, where they may also be susceptible to being hit by the falling droppings and regurgitated pellets of their social 'betters'.

Something similar seemed to be at work in the case of the ravens at Newborough. Wright and his colleagues were often able to identify by certain physical characteristics the individual ravens most often involved in recruitment behaviour. They could therefore confirm that these birds held a central location in the roost and were always the birds that recruited the others to the newly located sheep carcass. This was done through the performance of morning flights and calling displays above the roost. The authors agreed with Bernd Heinrich that there may be a social function for this recruitment behaviour. Young birds may gain prestige and dominance by advertising the whereabouts of food sources. The knowledgeable young raven could demonstrate their fitness as a partner and enhance their chances of gaining a mate and breeding successfully.

Could similar — or, indeed, other, quite different but nevertheless important — social processes be operating in rook/jackdaw roosts? I suspect they are. In fact I'd be shocked if they weren't. One of the best pieces of evidence I have centres once more on that wild downward flight mode I mentioned earlier, 'whiffling'. I said then that it looks like predator detection/avoidance behaviour. The reckless plunging trajectory would confuse any waiting bird of prey, and also possibly advertise that pursuit would be worthless because this was one rook/jackdaw in prime condition. But another striking aspect of whiffling is that it closely resembles the mode of flight rooks employ in what were once known among rural communities as 'crows' weddings'.

In these display flights, normally seen in autumn and early winter (in the Yare valley particularly on sunny September or October afternoons), rooks climb in wide circles on warm thermals. Then at a certain height, perhaps as much as 300–600 metres, the birds, usually in pairs or several pairs, tumble down through the airspace in a wild helter-skelter fashion. At the end of the crazy swoop, both rooks come close together in normal flight and resume their slow ascent once more. The performance is both beautiful to watch and absolutely typical of the mystery still surrounding this most conspicuous of species. There is little general agreement on the purpose of these manoeuvres, but the fact that they are performed simultaneously by two birds suggests to me that they have some association either with pair formation or as a bond-strengthening exercise for established couples. They look like birds in the act of showing off, displaying their super-fit flying abilities. They also look like acts of mutual co-ordination, a physical expression of emotional and psychological togetherness.

If whiffling and the flights performed in crows' weddings are structurally almost identical then why couldn't the sudden tumbling action so often witnessed when birds arrive at a roost have both functions: as social display and anti-predator strategy? To me it seems highly likely that they do. There may even be a third purpose. One other explanation for the whiffling flights into roosts is that they call attention to the existence of the roost itself: a social advertisement for the benefits of flocking.

I believe that there is even more evidence supporting the argument for whiffling's multiple function, because birds don't simply do it on arrival at roosts, they also do it when they rise at dawn on leaving. In these displays, the earliest birds fly above the trees then tumble back down close to the area from which they emerged. In such situations it may well be a further pre-emptive response to the danger from lurking birds of prey as a rook leaves the security of the roost. Yet it also looks like a summons from the first-risen and possibly dominant individuals to the laggards still clinging to the night-time perch. In short, this one kind of flight may have several simultaneous functions: while the emphasis shifts subtly with context, the flight always retains the potential for *all* of its various meanings.

It may not be just the whiffling into roosts that functions as a social display. Other aspects of the rooks' behaviour are equally intriguing. The element that most captivated my attention, the moment that first hooked me into the rooking life, was that occasion when I witnessed the birds' breathtaking collective flight at end of day, a cacophony of sound and energy boiling above the roost trees. The authors Ward and Zahavi suggested that this mushroom-cloud finale, which is audible from several kilometres and may well be visible, even in the gloaming, from a greater distance, is also a form of advertise- ment for the roost. It is a way of stating to other potential recruits: 'Come to our site, the bigger we are, the more successful you will be.' (This may well be the case but it strikes me that the occurrence of these 'marketing' activities in such low-light conditions doesn't really make as powerful an announcement as it might do.)

One other possible function is suggested to me by the moment which precedes it. In its way this preliminary action — or non-action, as the case may be — is as compelling an expression of collective unity as the maelstrom thereafter. It's that moment when all the rooks fall completely silent. Its singularity cannot be overstated. Throughout the entire assembly process, rook and jackdaw vocalisations are both continuous and completely without structure — an unceasing rook-racked din. Then this strange thing happens. All at once, after a period of physical concentration, with peripheral birds flying repeatedly towards a nominal centre, the entire flock goes quiet. In the previous chapter, where I described coming upon the roost flocks near Halleaths in Dumfriesshire and then again after my breathless cross-country chase from Somerleyton to Flixton Carr, the birds had arrived at this same uncanny stage of assembly. To witness a flock of large black birds, sometimes many thousands compressed into a dense blanket across the field, and utterly without sound, has a powerful effect.

I speculate whether this ritual silence, and the passionate vortex that follows it, have exactly the same function. Although they are opposites in terms of physical input, one a shared stillness, the other a chaos of flight and noise, they are identical in psychological requirement. They pitch each individual bird towards the collective heart. They reconcile the one to the flock. They attune the singleton — rook and jackdaw alike — to the processes of sociability which are at the very heart of its identity as a species. All the survival strategies and life processes of rooks and jackdaws depend upon collective behaviour. Perhaps these rituals at end of day are a way of binding them to that destiny, of knitting each individual bird into the shared fabric.

★   ★   ★

I've been studying corvid roosts now for more than six years. I don't believe for one moment that I understand even a third of what there is to know. Of this much, however, I am fairly sure. Zoologists propose that in the evolution of any bit of behaviour there is an initial survival benefit which triggers the first activity. In the case of corvid roosts it could be protection from predators or the elements, or its function as a food-information centre. One of these set corvids roosting and created the conditions in which secondary benefits evolved. Whichever may have been first, all of the above advantages have come to cement the importance of roosting in the lives of rooks and jackdaws. In addition there are other complex social processes operating in roosts. These may well include pair formation, displays of dominance, establishment of individual status within the flock, and even just the serious business of play — the psychological and physical benefits gained from recreational activity.

This complex matrix of interlocking advantages is hugely important to each individual bird. That realisation was powerfully reinforced for me when in the northern section of the Norfolk Broads I watched a small flock of jackdaws take flight from a derelict windmill at Horsey close to the coast. About forty minutes before dusk they passed over where I was standing, and disappeared to the south-west. When I plotted their course on the map, it was uncanny to find that 21 kilometres further along the same compass bearing their route coincided almost exactly with the large field where the birds gather before flying into Buckenham Carrs. I've calculated that rooks and jackdaws fly to roost at about 42 kilometres an hour. It means that those jackdaws spend thirty minutes on each journey and sixty minutes a day getting to and from their roost. Recall also that in midwinter their total feeding time might be reduced to just six hours. Yet they devote a significant proportion of that daylight to connecting with the roost. And that doesn't take account of the energy expended in the hour's flying time. For all that effort to be worth while, roosts must reward each bird with substantial dividends.

I'm sure that if I studied roosts for another six years I still wouldn't be able to work out what all those might be. Nor do I really mind that I shall never arrive at a definitive understanding. That was never my intended destination. The journey, in truth, has been everything.

17

In my opening chapter I stated that this book is an account of the vision summoned momentarily by the rooks and jackdaws as they fly to their roost at Buckenham Carrs. To quote my own words exactly, I said that it was about 'the elements of the natural world — the light, the environment, the birds, myself — which create it'.

The most perplexing part of that natural history, the subject which has lingered longest, is the last. It's the *me* of that moment which has proved the most elusive and impenetrable. In a sense I've become as puzzled by my deep preoccupation with roosting corvids as I have been beguiled by the birds themselves. I'm intrigued to know exactly where my fascination comes from, but more especially I want to work out how I should interpret it. Is it something deeply positive, or is it negative? Should I see it as a kind of failure? Does it imply a lack of something within me?

The questions took some time to surface. The rooks stole upon me so quickly and so completely that there seemed little time for self-reflection. Although I do remember my amusement once, when I got home from the marsh to find that there had been a phone call for me which Miriam had taken. 'No, sorry, Dad's out rooking,' she'd said, as if rooking was the kind of word and activity they'd understand in every household.

My first real inkling that it required consideration came when I rang my friend, the great writer on nature, Richard Mabey. He has an office in his garden and I'd phone sometimes and get the answering machine. Behind the words of his message I could dimly hear the calls of a corvid which must have been taped inadvertently as Richard made his recording. Initially I'd hoped it was a rook but I suspect it was a carrion crow. I told Richard about the bird; he replied, 'Gosh, Mark, you want to watch it. You're becoming a nerd.'

For me it was a joke with long antecedents. Even as a child I was wary of people discovering that I was a keen naturalist in case of the dreaded 'S' word. Sissy. In a previous book, *Birders: Tales of a Tribe*, I described the peculiar nature of this youthful anxiety. 'I often rehearsed a nightmare scenario in which a large gang of girls stood in a scornful huddle laughing at the nerd with the binoculars. I don't know why I should have had that particular childhood fantasy. At that age I didn't even know any girls.'

The same problem has resurfaced occasionally in adult life. When *Birders* was published I got an invitation to appear on the television programme, *The Big Breakfast*. At first I thought it was a great bit of media exposure for the book, but Jonathan Cape's publicity officer pleaded with me *not* to do it. I was only being asked, she said, so that Johnny Vaughan, the host, could take the piss.

The issue isn't restricted to naturalists. My elder daughter Rachael is passionate about music and drama. She loves to create films with our digital camera and to perform short plays with her sister and cousins. One of her teenage friends, who shares none of these interests (or talents, perhaps), told her that she was weird. The 'S' word is no longer 'sissy'; in these contemporary exchanges it's 'sad'.

But why is it that people who are absorbed by something are seen as sad? And what licenses that particular remark? What strange presumption fortifies the unengaged and the dispassionate to express this scorn for the enthusiast? I was mystified. So I went in search of people who were themselves equally passionate, equally obsessive, perhaps equally sad — I hope they will forgive the idea — as myself.

★ ★ ★

Derek Ratcliffe (1929–2005), was one of the finest British naturalists in the second half of the last century and, according to some, the most complete all-rounder since Charles Darwin. It's a claim not easily disputed. Derek edited and largely wrote the *Nature Conservation Review*, a two-volume inventory of the country's richest landscapes and a framework document that shaped much of official environmental policy in the last thirty years. His speciality was uplands, on whose flora he was an expert. He wrote natural histories of two highly distinctive stretches of hill country, Dumfries and Galloway and the Lake District, his home territory. During the course of his early years in the Nature Conservancy, for whom he eventually served as Chief Scientist, he acquired a deep intimacy with many of the most remote, wild and lonely places in Britain. A favourite was the waterlogged peat bogs of Sutherland and Caithness in far northern Scotland, whose popular name — the Flow Country — Derek coined.

He loved these fragments of wilderness for their own sake but he also loved them because they were the last refuge of his life's guiding stars, two quintessential upland inhabitants, the peregrine and raven. In his scrupulous, spare, lucid prose Derek wrote monographs on both birds, the former book widely recognised as a model of the single-species study.

His love of peregrines and ravens acquired its particular shape under the tutelage of Ernest Blezard, curator of the museum in Derek's home town, Carlisle. The older naturalist stood at the centre of a coterie of tough northern birdmen, some of whom had been or were still occasional egg collectors. Certainly all were nest visitors, birdmen who loved to get on close terms with the most secret and intimate details in the lives of these elusive crag-dwelling species. Their speciality was to risk life and limb climbing, often with ropes in pairs or teams, to the cliff eyries of nesting ravens and peregrines. Derek acquired that need in full measure.

When I went to visit him at his Cambridge home he was already in his seventies, a lean, chaste figure of frugal habits and carefully selected words. The peregrine fixation was now largely behind him as an active pursuit, although he had extensively updated his book, *The Peregrine*, in 1993, thirteen years after it was first published. The far north of Scandinavia, Lapland, had latterly become the pre-eminent joy in Derek's life. He visited every year for fourteen summers, May to

July, from 1990 to 2004, completing the 4,000-kilometre round journey with his wife Jeanette in their camper van. The vehicle was in his Cambridge drive when he came out to greet me.

It was about his earliest years as a naturalist, when Derek acquired his visceral attachments, that I most wanted to hear. I should add that his passion for finding the nests of peregrines and ravens and, if possible, viewing their contents was blended within a scrupulous regard for the well-being of his quarry. No individual in the country did more to rescue peregrines from their calamitous pesticide-driven decline in the 1950s and 1960s. It was Derek's work that eventually forced the withdrawal of DDT and, subsequently, the organochlorine pesticides that were at the root of the falcon's problems.

When he first began his quest for the nest sites all across the southern uplands, from Galloway in the west right through to the Cheviots in Northumberland, he could have had no idea of its eventual outcome, nor of the deeply constructive and important purpose which it would acquire. That, in a sense, touches upon the essence of his love-affair with the bird. It had no final goal. It was an end in itself.

As Derek talked I could sense the electric

current of feeling he had had for being close to this most talismanic of British birds. When he was forced to move away from peregrine country because of his conservation work elsewhere, he described how he often burned to get back to the hills. Annually he devoted part of his leave simply to checking the nest sites that he had long known. In the end the round of calls acquired the character of a family visit, a dutiful tour of distant relatives, to monitor their fortunes and catch up on breeding successes crag by crag.

Many of the foundations for this work had been established when he was a teenager and undergraduate. The story I cherish most as an index of Derek's commitment to his totem species comes in the most personal of his books, *In Search of Nature*, which serves as a sort of ecological autobiography and is as near to self-revelation as this intensely shy man ever came. It describes an excursion he made in April 1952 when he took a train to Hexham and then continued by pushbike to complete a round tour of three raven nests that he wanted to see. To his bitter disappointment all three sites had been robbed of their eggs by collectors. As Derek wrote,

It was a poor reward for perhaps the hardest day I ever did — 12 miles on the hill and 90 miles on the bike. I well remember the gruelling cycle ride, round by the Liddel head and back by Newcastleton, for there was a strong west wind, not far off gale force, against which I battled most of the day. Back home late in the evening, I slumped on the bed and fell fast asleep. My mother called me for supper, but I was out for the count.

It's not just his physical stamina that leaves me gasping. Rooks are everywhere in Norfolk. If I wanted to, I could watch them all day and every day. But I know from my eighteen years in Derbyshire what it's like to be in barren upland landscapes. In April, birds — any birds — are low in diversity and few in number. I can recall outings when I saw just six species; perhaps 1–2 individuals of each. Derek's attachment was to not just the most charismatic of upland birds but to two of the rarest and most elusive. Devotion to the peregrine and the raven demanded long spells of little but the sour wind, the steep gradient, the steady iamb of a pounding heart, interrupted now and then by a few minutes, sometimes only seconds, of fulfilment. It speaks of a deep, obdurate commitment and it fills me with awe.

Superficially Derek Ratcliffe and Desmond Nethersole Thompson (1908–1989) seem opposites in almost every regard. While one was small and slight, the other was physically large, robust and in his youth a gifted light-heavyweight boxer. While Derek was emotionally reserved and socially wary, Desmond was a raconteur, a voraciously curious conversationalist and a lover of argument, even rancour. For twenty years he was a fiery socialist councillor who stood unsuccessfully for parliament in 1950 and again in 1955.

The Labour Party's loss was undoubtedly ornithology's gain, because Desmond was also one of the most gifted students of bird behaviour. Like Ratcliffe he specialised in a handful of species, writing monographs on three rare inhabitants of the Scottish Highlands, *The Snow Bunting* (1966), *The Dotterel* (1973) and *Pine Crossbills* (1975). As an author he shared Ratcliffe's attention to detail but their styles couldn't have been more different. Derek's was quiet, restrained, detached. Desmond found writing a real trial, yet he managed to infuse his sentences about nest behaviour and courtship display with some of his intense feelings for birds. It led to a curious tension in his behavioural studies. At one level the books are highly technical pieces of objective observation, and on another they are instinct with his tender and impassioned engagement in the lives of his subjects. You can almost imagine this great bear of a man with these enormously fragile birds cradled in his large light-heavyweight's paws. Very few if any other ornithological writers have managed this balance of forensic detail and emotional involvement. It brought Nethersole Thompson huge acclaim and his books are still acknowledged as classics.

Yet Desmond is perhaps most remarkable for his singular devotion to one species. The love of his life, on which he wrote not one but two book-length studies — the second with his wife Maimie — was a tall slim long-legged beauty called *Tringa nebularia*, the white-rumped wader of the mist, the greenshank. There was a faintly scandalous edge to this grand passion, because it arose in part from his dubious affairs as a youth. The young Desmond — and some even accused the middle-aged man — had been an egg collector. The greenshank was universally acknowledged by the oological community (a title eggers sometimes claim for themselves to supply the gloss of scientific respectability) as their blue riband bird, quite simply because the nest is so damn difficult to find. The severity of this contest appealed to Nethersole Thompson's competitive pugilist instinct and he devoted decades to unravelling the mysteries of the greenshank's love life.

Ironically it was Derek Ratcliffe who first discovered the location where Desmond would bring his passion for the species to its fullest expression: the sodden oozy bogs that lie in the twin shadow of Cranstackie and Foinaven in far north-westernmost Scotland. During a chance visit in 1957 Derek recognised that the bird was commoner in this part of Sutherland than anywhere else he had ever been. In fact, it has some of the highest greenshank densities found anywhere in the world.

It was one thing to listen to the song-flight and watch the displays of adults. It was another entirely to track these prospective parents to their nest with its clutch of beautiful, olive or buff-toned chocolate-ornamented eggs. Greenshank breed out on the flows in an infinity of sameness. To find the nest you can track the non-sitting bird from its feeding pool when it finally returns to relieve its incubating partner. But the foraging site could be anything from three kilometres, sometimes as much as thirteen kilometres, from the precise bowl of grasses on which its mate is sitting. Their change of guard duties can take place in the blink of an eye. To miss it could mean the negation of twelve hours' hard search. Sometimes it can take a week of barely contained frustration to locate one nest.

Desmond went about this formidable task by setting up residence at the foot of Cranstackie every spring from 1962 onwards for the next twenty years. Home from late April to mid-June was a tiny fishing hut on the banks of the River Dionard. It would have been a claustrophobic squeeze for Desmond and Maimie by themselves, but as their family started to expand there was never any notion of the children being denied the challenge of the greenshank. At its peak there were eight of them shoehorned into that minuscule 4 x 3-metre wooden structure listening to the river's song each night. Their camp stood seven kilometres from the nearest road and thirty-two from the nearest shop; there was no fresh food but what they could store, no fresh water but what they drew from the stream and no human company except each other. For six weeks children and adults were locked into the intimate embrace of Dionard. Yet all are agreed that it was not so much a prison as a paradise of natural purity, a unique and unforgettable experience in a landscape barely changed since the last Ice Age. The unanimous view is that Maimie's genius for organisation underpinned the entire adventure; her quartermaster duties for the annual stint at the camp began as early as January. On site it was she who did the cooking, packed the lunches, took the daily log in shorthand and looked after the little ones around the camp.

Desmond's contribution was to inspire the longest continuous study programme not simply of greenshank but of any wader community anywhere in the world. The children continue it even now. Many of the individual birds they came to know by name. Their family fortunes and breeding successes they followed intimately and in detail sometimes for as long as twelve years. In the end they thought of the birds as people. As friends. The fact that this study was completed in partnership by the Thompson family unit of eight makes it one of the most remarkable stories in British ornithology.

Three of the children eventually matched their father and acquired Ph.D.s. Derek Ratcliffe, however, from whom compliments were not drawn cheaply, thought Thompson senior the most brilliant student of nesting birds he'd ever met. That talent lay mainly in a single uncomplicated quality. Patience.

Quite simply Desmond out-sat, out-waited and out-thought his greenshank, and I like to imagine this exceptional man on those flows, his solid frame stooped forward in a posture of dogged concentration. The outer context is nothing more than a cloud race across the heavens and a brown waste of bog below; but the inner scene is subtle and balletic, a human mind shadow-boxing with the will-o'-the-wisp moods of his beloved bird.

★   ★   ★

John Buxton (1913–1989), Peter Conder (1919–1993), and George Waterston (1911–1980) were a deeply impressive trio of birdmen. The first became a distinguished Oxford don and poet; the other two ranked among the leading environmentalists of their age. Yet when they conducted the ornithological study in which I'm interested, the three cut a rather sorrier figure. They were hollow-cheeked, ragged and down at heel young men, while at least one, George Waterston, was in chronic ill health. Even the study, with which they will be forever associated, was a rather paltry affair. The final paper, a sixteen-page note, was light on results and thin on methodology. It's primary author, M.J. Waterhouse, has vanished almost completely from the record, and nothing else he has written has come to light. In any other context I doubt that this paper would even have been published. But, then, that context I mention is virtually everything.

The piece appeared in the journal of the British Ornithologists' Union, *Ibis*, in 1949 and was entitled 'Rook and Jackdaw Migrations Observed in Germany, 1942–1945'. Waterhouse, like his three collaborators, was a prisoner of war, and their collective study of the autumn passage by European corvids was a means of whiling away the achingly dull months and years of confinement. The scientific portion of the paper can be summarised very briefly. In autumn, rooks and jackdaws leave north-eastern Europe for warmer climes further west. Come spring, the pattern is reversed. Buxton, Conder and Waterston noticed this and, together with a floating pool of co-opted helpers, they kept count of the birds flying directly over their various POW camps. At the end of the war they were able to compare the figures obtained from different parts of Hitler's Greater Germany and draw a few rough conclusions about numbers, seasonality, direction of migration, flight altitude and flock formation.

At their peak the various volunteers were devoting most of their daylight hours to counting crows. Buxton, Conder and Waterston, at Dössel, were watching from 7.30 in the morning until seven at night. In thirty-nine dark days during March and April 1942, with Singapore newly fallen and with the Axis forces lured by Pyrrhic victories — Rommel at Tobruk and von Paulus in Stalingard — to over-extension and then ultimate defeat, these British birdmen logged a total of 39,000 rooks and jackdaws in the skies above their prison.

The paper might not be notable for its ornithological content, but as a document on human resourcefulness and imagination in the most trying circumstances it is outstanding. And as a piece of testimony about national characteristics it's a classic. It is hard to imagine it appearing in the scientific literature of any other country. One or two of the insouciant little asides in the text are absolutely priceless. For instance, in a section listing the systematic nature of observations that were made at Dössel, Waterhouse adds, 'except when unavoidably prevented by activities of the Germans'. In a similar piece describing how the counts were made at Eichstätt camp it notes: 'same methods continued in spring but much interrupted by air-raids'.

Perhaps my all-time favourite is based on information supplied by Peter Conder, who was a second lieutenant in the Royal Corps of

Signals before he was caught at St Valéry-sur-Somme in June 1940. Conder's years of incarceration narrowed his focus to what might entice jackdaws and rooks to stop and feed in the course of their trans-European journeys. To give us insight into the habits of the briefly delayed migrants, Waterhouse, citing Conder's observations, listed a trio of feeding hotspots. One was the camp rubbish dump where the birds loved to fossick in paper bags. Another choice location was 'Fields newly spread with human excrement'.

I must confess I can't read these fragments without pain-edged amusement, or without imagining the ironic smile on the face of their author or the faces of his three top contributors. Behind each of the tiny remarks is a whole library of inferential material on the nature of war and incarceration, on the protocols governing scientific text, on British understatement and on the old masculine need for casualness in matters of distaste, fear, danger and even mortality.

The *Ibis* paper is a wonderful bit of ornithological history. It is important to me not so much for its revelations about obsession — although many may well see daily, twelve-hour counts of migrating rooks while the world tore itself to pieces as clear evidence of obsession — but for the insights it offers into how the watching of birds might function for all of its devotees. You cannot encounter these descriptions of migration in the heavens above wartime Europe and not imagine how it worked on the spirits of these half-starved, temporarily defeated and ultimately redeemed men. Perhaps all monomanias share something of the characteristics so poignantly outlined here. They are a way of offsetting some deeper pain in life.

★ ★ ★

I have one last example of devotion to a single species to recount before I attempt to assess what they all mean and how they function. It brings me right back to my core theme, because it concerns the earliest ever long-term study of the rook, probably anywhere in the world. It was first brought to light in Andrew Lanyon's curious and intriguing photographic collection entitled *The Rooks of Trelawne*, and subsequently by Franklin Coombs in his book, *The Crows*.

The study was by a Victorian figure called Lewis Harding and was prescribed as a form of therapy by Jonathan Couch, a notable Cornish naturalist and also Harding's medical doctor. In 1846 Harding had newly returned from eleven years in the Antipodes in what Couch described as 'a very imperfect state of health'. He had then taken up residence in a house called Trelawne near the tiny hamlet of Pelynt and owned by his wealthy uncle, Sir Harry Trelawny. This ancient property was surrounded by a huge rookery of almost 500 nests and Couch put his invalid to work watching the birds and maintaining a weekly, then monthly account of their activities. This was eventually assembled as a bound volume of notes.

It is Andrew Lanyon who offers the only insight into why Trelawne's convalescent rook-watcher had been so emotionally and spiritually scarred by his time overseas. The young man had gone out to Australia in 1835 to teach in a Catholic seminary in Sydney, but in 1840 he had been transferred to a post on Norfolk Island. It was almost certainly Harding's five years in this South Pacific nightmare that triggered his mental break-down.

Norfolk Island is a pinprick about 800 kilometres north-west of New Zealand's northernmost tip and 1,800 kilometres east of Sydney. In 1840 few places on Earth were more beastly. In the Australian colony, whose founding rationale was to serve as a cloaca for the human effluent adrift in the streets of Georgian England, Norfolk Island operated as the final and inescapable sump. It was where the transported felons were sent if they had been reconvicted during their penal servitude in Australia. According to the colonial administrator charged with its establishment, Norfolk Island was to be 'the *ne plus ultra* of convict degradation'.

For more than a decade the system on Norfolk had been managed by sadists as a hell-hole of overwork underscored by a regime of violent punishment. It was not the sort of place to soothe the moral conscience of a devoutly religious young man. But Harding's mental collapse may have been precipitated not simply by contact with this kind of barbarism. He had arrived on Norfolk at the same moment as a reforming governor called Alexander Maconochie. This high-minded administrator instituted a massive overhaul of the worst aspects of the system and achieved rapid improvements in both the behaviour and the spirit of his charges. Unfortunately Maconochie's enlightened regime was not to the liking of the bigots on the Australian mainland, for whom the purpose of Norfolk Island was to inflict pain and punishment, not to reform.

Having seen what might be achieved through the application of fairness, reason and simple human decency, Lewis Harding had the peculiar misfortune to remain on Norfolk while Maconochie's reforms were cancelled one by one and the system returned to its old sadistic formula. In the year of Harding's eventual departure, one visiting churchman calculated that the new governor had administered over 26,000 lashes upon his charges in twelve months. The whipping post where the torture was inflicted was as 'saturated with human gore as if a bucket of blood had been spilled on it, covering a space of three feet in diameter and running out in various directions in little streams two or three feet long'. By 1845 the emotionally shattered Harding could presumably stand it no longer.

When he returned to Trelawne house in 1846 he was described as 'a great invalid', but he was at least fortunate to have Jonathan Couch as the family doctor. As well as being Polperro's devoted physician, Couch was a prolific contributor to scientific journals and passionately engaged with most aspects of local Cornish life. When he met Harding he was already the father of five adult children, three of whom were also doctors. In 1858 Couch, aged sixty-nine, married a third time and had three more children. In *The Rooks of Trelawne*, Andrew Lanyon speculates that the library of this intellectually omnivorous man must have included a translation of a recent French study of insanity. In this, the author, Philippe Pinel, recommended that sufferers of nervous disorder should be engaged in some appropriate and rewarding activity. Couch's occupational therapy for the forty-one-year-old Harding was to set him rooking.

Harding's final therapeutic document was compiled over 1847–48 and comprised twelve sections, including a chronological diary of his rook observations coupled with a monthly summary, August to August. As Franklin Coombs writes, it was remarkable both for its detail and its accuracy. Harding was one of the first to record many intimate aspects of the bird's social life, and his findings were all the more impressive given that he had very little literature to help him interpret the raw information. However, as in the case of Waterston's *Ibis* paper of 1949, I am less interested in the ornithological content of Harding's journal than in the human story behind it.

Andrew Lanyon felt that Harding's gradual mental recovery could be seen both in the markedly improved character of his handwriting as the journal unfolds, and in the sheer quality and organisation evident in the later writings, which have an almost professional exactitude. Further proof of Harding's recovery is that he eventually moved to Polperro and died there, aged eighty-seven, in 1893. He seems to have pursued no more systematic natural-historical work, but he did acquire the necessary chemical, engineering and aesthetic insights to become highly skilled in the pioneer art of photography. His images of everday Cornish life in the mid-Victorian period, which are profiled in Lanyon's book, now form an important historical collection.

★   ★   ★

In the life stories of any of these striking and varied people — Derek Ratcliffe, Desmond Nethersole Thompson, John Buxton, Peter Conder, George Waterston and Lewis Harding — one can discern two fundamental human drives. The first is quite simple. It's unquenchable curiosity or, in the case of Lewis Harding, the healing, creative power of curiosity. In *The Act of Creation*, the second volume in his huge tripartite study of the human mind, Arthur Koestler argued that being inquisitive is not simply a defining characteristic of a single highly evolved primate. It is a condition of all living things. It is evident in the kitten playing with a ball of string, or the puppy tumbling in play-fight with its siblings, and even — perhaps especially — in the example cited by Darwin in *The Descent of Man*. Monkeys have an intense dread of snakes that is almost but not quite as powerful as their insatiable curiosity. In laboratory conditions where the reptiles were kept in a lidded box, the monkeys, in the most human fashion possible, couldn't resist lifting up the lid to remind themselves of the object of their terror.

Koestler argued that this appetite for exploring the outer world was not just intended to support other intrinsic drives such as the need to find food or to reproduce. Curiosity was an end in itself: in Koestler's words, 'the motivation for learning is to learn'. Quoting the Cambridge psychologist Kenneth Craik, he proposed that the function of curiosity was to create an interior map of the external world. This small-scale, portable model of outer reality allows the organism to trial and compare alternative versions and in the end to find ways of reacting to life that are more efficient and safer. Koestler concluded:

Thus the organism functions not merely by responding to the environment, but by asking it questions. The main incentive to its exploratory activities are novelty, surprise, conflict, uncertainty. The exploratory drive may combine with, or be instrumental to, other drives — sex, nutrition, and anxiety. But in its purest form — in play, latent learning, unrewarded problem-solving — 'stimuli' and 'responses' are undistinguishable parts of the same feedback loop along which excitation is running in a circle like a kitten chasing its tail.

Asking questions of our natural environment has been central to human evolution for more than three million years. Contemporary science is simply a more precise and codified form of an investigation initiated when we first rose up off all fours on the African savannah. Only perhaps in living memory have many members of contemporary society been able to forget completely the ecological context which nourished and sustained every previous generation of our ancestors.

Although the process of looking seems to set up opposition between the observer and the observed, humans remain part of that context, the very field of their observational studies. Moreover, the American naturalist Edward O. Wilson argues that that sense of relatedness is itself innate. We feel an instinctive empathy for our surroundings. All of the characters I listed and described above were compelled by this second dominant drive. Wilson's word for it is *biophilia*: a love of life. So not only is the drive to enquire part of the very essence of what it means to be alive, as Koestler argues; according to Wilson, we also feel deeply and positively for the thing we investigate. To fuse the two drives together, therefore, enquiring becomes a way of loving.

To peg your love of life upon the study of a single species can be a way of shutting the rest out, a retreat from complexity, a reduction of the whole sunlit panorama to a simple vista. But what, at times, is wrong with that? It can be a deeply restorative process, as in the case of Lewis Harding, obliterating the shame and horror of his past in the intoxicating plume of birds above his Cornish home. It may also be a kind of wisdom, as shown by Buxton, Conder and Waterston, incarcerated British birdmen watching rooks in a square of sky like black stars across the German heavens.

To return briefly to my earlier question: why is it that people who are absorbed by something are seen as sad? I can't explain it, but for me it reverses the true state of affairs. To be engaged is to be a part, to be absorbed and fulfilled. To be cool, to be detached from things and to have no passionate feeling is the real sadness. At the heart of depression, that quintessentially modern malaise, is a deep sense of separation from the rest of life.

At its fullest, studying the life of another living creature is a way of engaging all of your faculties. In short, it's a way of being intensely alive, and recognising that you are so. At the same time it is a form of valuing life and of appreciating *the* fundamental tenet of all ecology: that every thing is connected to everything else. So I would argue that rooking isn't merely about a single raucous black bird. It is about the whole world — the landscape, the sunlight, the very oxygen we share — all that lies between myself and the bird.

Reflecting on his encounters with another species, Edward Wilson, whose whole life has been a world-changing odyssey in search of the ant, expressed it thus:

The naturalist's journey has only just begun and for all intents and purposes will go on forever. That it is possible to spend a lifetime in a magellanic voyage around the trunk of a single tree. That as the exploration is pressed, it will engage more of the things close to the human heart and spirit. And if this much is true, it seems possible that the naturalist's vision is only a specialized product of a biophilic instinct shared by all, that it can be elaborated to benefit more and more people. Humanity is exalted not because we are far above other living creatures, but because knowing them well elevates the very concept of life.

18

Against the wider silence of the house, my creaking footfalls on the landing seem almost noisy and I engage with my first thought of the day, a slight pang of guilt. I must slip away quietly so as not to wake the girls. As the idea arrives the night presses in for the first time on my naked body and for the first time I notice how cold it is. I've instantly lost the warm, soft, slumped atmosphere of our bedroom, with its faintly acrid odour of sleep, and where Mary's unconscious body is still cocooned in its own slender mould among the bedclothes.

I look out of the bathroom window to the north, towards Buckenham Carrs, and I can tell the dawn is coming. My birds will soon be coming with it, across the fields and over the house. I want to be at the Yare when they first set off so that I can measure the light and record their various directions away from the roost. It's one of my dawn excursions for rooks and I'm pleased that I've timed it perfectly.

Back in the bedroom I wrestle on a pair of faded beige combat trousers. Then comes a thick pair of home-knitted socks, which I pull over the legs of the trousers, so my feet will run easily into the wellies. As I order the hose of the socks against the combats I'm already imagining my return to the house. I can see the girls laughing at this outfit, teasing me about my appearance. They call these trousers my 'frogs', because they say that the cut of them — the baggy tops and tight-fitting calves — makes me look like the creature in question. As I take my tea and muesli to the dining room, gently fatigued from my pre-dawn excursion, the two sisters will amuse themselves at their dad's rooking gear and what their friends would think of his 'frogs' and his silly socks.

By the time I've imagined all this I'm ready to go. I open the front door and immediately a whole other world comes flooding up, achieving contact in that delicious smack of cold night air. I pull up the zip on my down jacket (known affectionately to the girls as 'puffer') and I am at once in a state of perfect equilibrium with the new place. Even in the pre-dawn light, with its rudimentary realm of grey shapes, things start to assume their customary order.

Most satisfying is the robin. By January its song is a fixture of this time of the day. It bubbles up out of the black mass of our hedge like a tiny breeze-ruffled brook of notes. I can fix it best by imagining it as a colour — a trembling line of silver in the darkness. That rinsing watery sound, with its insinuating power, seems so perfectly matched to this portion of the year and even through the growl of the car engine I can hear it still. It's the first god of the morning.

The second is entirely unexpected. It feels like — it is — a benediction. A tawny owl, bound for some dark ivy-clad spot in the woods at the back of the village, has chosen exactly that moment to perch on a fence post out in the open as I drive past. The car headlights cleave it briefly clean out of the darkness. It has the power of an apparition.

It bobs its head, adjusting the angle of focus slightly, tilting those liquid dark eyes the better to weigh the moment, and with all the power at its disposal it does that bird thing: and the instant of take-off, that fragment of a second when it launches itself into space, pushing down with those steel-clawed feet, the brown wings unfurling, the primaries running out, one by one, over the secondaries and resting as a single interlocking membrane on the gentle slope of the night breeze, seems to go on for ever.

In an owl-induced reverie I can see it perfectly in my mind's eye as I drive along.

The rest of the short journey is a blur and as I crunch the gravel down the track to the Yare I am aware of the night already melting away to the east. On the bank itself I look downstream and the river appears as a broad twisted sheet of tin, meandering away on its own non-existent gradient. There are some mute swans and one lumbers into flight, the great feet spanking the river as it heaves into the air. I count the footfalls — twenty-seven dying beats upon the water — before it finally rises clear of the Earth. Flying mute swans are not particularly graceful birds but they have a certain heraldic power and by the time it's passing overhead the roost is awake.

The first rooks come up out of the woods. They're little more than distant specks. They rise up then instantly tumble down, careening madly over the trees, some even returning to their perch. But the action seems to trigger more and more birds to rise. By the time a great plume of rooks and jackdaws has mushroomed up over Buckenham, a first jackdaw is even passing by me, high and quiet and purposeful.

The breaking apart of the Buckenham roost has a rather hectic air, in contrast to the measured formality of its evening assembly. The whole body of birds never rises as one, in the way that they do at dusk, but the exodus of most of the flock spans just fifteen minutes. At its height, huge numbers boil up into a great dishevelled cavalcade, turning back upon itself now and then as if to summon further recruits but always spinning slowly south towards the river. I often wish I could see the whole thing from above, so that one could appreciate all of these radial lines of birds pulsing outwards like shock waves from an epicentre.

The one infallible element in the roost's disintegration is the joyous hubbub of the birds' calls, which seem instilled with a sense of the day's new beginning. The mood continues even as they fly over our house, several minutes to the south, and as they pass over me now, I wonder if they will shortly penetrate the dreamy recesses of Mary's sleeping head. I find the mood of the birds contagious and suspect sometimes I come down simply to get my fix of this irrepressible spirit. I get out my camera to take the shutter speed in various parts of the sky. I note the time and the volume of the birds passing south, as well as the other directions which the flocks are taking. I'm not certain what value there is in my observations, but I'm too immersed in the moment to care, and then I get the reward for my morning's efforts.

It lasts about thirty seconds — the time it

takes to follow a large, loose flock of birds heading downstream. As my eye travels with them eastwards I become aware of the light behind turning from deep lemon to a wonderful rich pink that floods the whole horizon. The black silhouetted birds passing through these improbably bright colours remind me instantly of a scene I saw once while rooking at Garlieston in south-west Scotland.

It was an unusual roost. The birds gather in the oak and pine fringing the grounds of Galloway House. The spot stands barely a hundred metres from the rocky coastline of Wigtown Bay, so that for once the corvids' water-on-stone calls mingle with the lullaby sounds of a genuine tide. Most of the roost occupants come from the north and in the last stretch of their approach they're forced to sail down from the heights at Eggerness Point out across the open water in Garlieston's picturesque bay. I positioned myself by the abandoned factory on the old pier head to catch this southerly flow. The air was absolutely still, the mirror surface of the sea blurred by a faint mist, while the smoke lines rising from the seaside cottages sailed vertically into a starlit sky. Down the rooks came through the ice blue, across the lemon white above the hills of Galloway and finally deep down into the deep peach light above the roost.

It was magical, and all of this comes to me as I stand on the banks of the Yare. I realise as I move from the memory to the moment that this is one of the great gifts of rooking. My experiences have now piled up into deep layers that infuse my sense of things, not just here in the Yare valley, but everywhere. Each occasion has its host of secondary reflections, a recessional of other times and other places. Just as the flight lines of the rooks interlace this country, so my pursuit of them has drawn the whole landscape together as one distinct place.

I scrabble quickly in my coat pocket for my notebook before all of this vanishes and I find nestled there in the very corner my little lens of black flint. It occurs to me as I ponder this last minute of my morning's excursion that it is impossible to make something as hard and enduring as this jewel in my hand. Nor can I recreate anything as beautiful or perfect as this blue-and-apricot crow morning by the Yare. Yet perhaps I should make a start . . . and so here it is.

Acknowledgements

The nineteenth-century naturalist Alfred Newton thought that 'A good monograph of the rook could not fail to be as interesting as its compilation would be laborious.' This is not a monograph of the rook, but then nor has it in any sense been laborious to write, partly because all sorts of people have shown great willingness to be enthusiastic about the project. I wish to express my deep gratitude to them under the following headings and apologise deeply for any omissions:

Sources of information
Mr and Mrs Michael Aylmer, David Ballance, Colin Beckett, Tom Beevor, Professor Tim Birkhead, Nigel Brown, John Cantelo, Rod Chapman, Joe Cullen, Julie Curl, Mike Densley, Billy Driver, Giles Dunmore, Graham Easy, Jonas Elleströms, Dodge Engleman, Mike Everett, Clive Fairweather, Clem Fisher, Graham Ford, Chris Goldsmith, Chris Gomersall, Adam Gretton, N. F. Howard, Ernest Hoyos, Tony Irwin, Kathleen Jamie, Andy Jarrett, Pat Kavanagh, Bill Landells, Nigel Larkin, Martin Limbert, Arthur Livett,

Roger Lovegrove, Lucy Luck, Richard Mabey, Mike McCarthy, Ole Malmberg, John Marchant, Tim Melling, Lennart Nilsson, Nigel Odin, Dr Stephen Piper, Katrina Porteous, Ralf Ramm, the late Derek and Jeanette Ratcliffe, Nigel Redman, Roger Riddington, Robin Sellers, David Simpson, Derek Skilling, Tony Stones, Denis Summers-Smith, Des Thompson, Maimie (Nethersole) Thompson, Pat Thompson, Sylvia Took, G. Went, Jim Whitaker, K. Widd, Olive Willis, Ruth Wood, Martin Woodcock, John Young. Ian Dawson and Lynn Giddings were my guides at the RSPB Library, while Graham Appleton and other staff members gave assistance at the Nunnery, the offices of the British Trust for Ornithology. I also thank Alice Brotherton and Neil Moffat at Dumfries Library, Catherine Littlejohn of Gressenhall Rural Life Museum, and the staff at Loddon and Norwich Libraries. Finally two great polymaths of the bird world, Jonathan Elphick and Ken Spencer, require extra special thanks for chasing down and sending me such a wide sweep of rook-related materials.

Hosts and companions
Stephen Culley acted as an invaluable guide to Tony and Adam Hare and myself when we visited the Newborough raven roost on

Anglesey. Colin Beckett provided excellent companionship during a visit to Hatton Castle, Aberdeenshire, while its owner David James Duff kindly gave us access to the estate. John and Clare Fanshawe were the perfect hosts in Cornwall, even arranging for rooks to build a nest above my bedroom at their house in Boscastle. My friends Paul and Liz Lewis gave me accommodation during my research at the RSPB headquarters in Sandy, while the residents of Pelican House, Redmond, Belinda and Galen O'Hanlon, were over-generous hosts during my visit to the Edward Grey Institute in Oxford.

Inner circle
All books have an inner circle. My agent Gill Coleridge and editor Dan Franklin are an indispensable double act and have been at the heart of almost everything I've written. I give them renewed thanks on our fifth book together. I also thank the other members of the outstanding Cape team, including Alex Bowler (Editorial), Anna Crone (Design) and Laura Hassan (Publicity). I owe a massive debt, personal and professional, to my good friend Tim Dee: for his wonderful company in Norfolk, Scotland, Spain and Turkey, for the wisdom of his advice throughout and, rarest of all, for his gift of intelligent and

creative conversation. 'My girls' — my partner, Mary, and our daughters, Rachael and Milly — have been there from the very first day of this adventure. For their good humour, their deep tolerance and, in a strange but profound way, for never having bothered to go rooking more than once, I give heartfelt thanks and love.

We do hope that you have enjoyed reading this large print book.

Did you know that all of our titles are available for purchase?

We publish a wide range of high quality large print books including:
Romances, Mysteries, Classics
General Fiction
Non Fiction and Westerns

Special interest titles available in large print are:
The Little Oxford Dictionary
Music Book
Song Book
Hymn Book
Service Book

Also available from us courtesy of Oxford University Press:
Young Readers' Dictionary
(large print edition)
Young Readers' Thesaurus
(large print edition)

For further information or a free brochure, please contact us at:
Ulverscroft Large Print Books Ltd.,
The Green, Bradgate Road, Anstey,
Leicester, LE7 7FU, England.
Tel: **(00 44) 0116 236 4325**
Fax: **(00 44) 0116 234 0205**

Other titles published by
The House of Ulverscroft:

IN THE KEY OF GENIUS

Adam Ockelford

Derek Paravicini is blind and autistic with severe learning difficulties but has a rare gift — he is a musical prodigy whose piano-playing has thrilled audiences from Ronnie Scott's, to Buckingham Palace. As a baby, given a toy organ, he began to teach himself to play. Music proved to be his means of expression and communication. At the age of four he was already an exceptional musician in the making. His mentor, and music psychologist Dr Adam Ockelford's account is a testament to the young man who can't tell his right hand from his left, yet amazes his audiences.

LET ME EAT CAKE

Paul Arnott

When Paul Arnott was a boy his mother gave him sugar and melted butter for a sore throat; his first love was Tate & Lyle's Golden Syrup. A collector of sweet sensations, he has sampled Vienna's many sachertortes, taken tea at Buckingham Palace and visited Hershey, the town built by the chocolate magnate. But this is also the story of a man who has grown horizontally and begun to wobble at the sides — a fact that led to a season as Father Christmas. Yet Paul feels no regret: *Let Me Eat Cake* is a memoir celebrating the experiences that caused every extra pound.

BORN ON A BLUE DAY

Daniel Tammet

Daniel sees numbers as shapes and colours and can perform extraordinary maths in his head. He can also learn to speak a language fluently in a week. For Daniel has Savant Syndrome, a rare form of Asperger's that gives him extraordinary mental powers, similar to the 'Rain Man' portrayed by Dustin Hoffman. Daniel has a compulsive need for order and routine — he eats exactly 45 grams of porridge for breakfast and counts the number of items of clothing he's wearing. But, unlike the 'Rain Man' and most people with severe autistic disorders, he is able to live a fully independent life. It is his incredible self-awareness and his ability to communicate what it feels like to live in a unique way that makes his story so powerful.